FAVORITE FISH & SEAFOOD RECIPES

by
John Davis

Illustrated by
Kevin Carter

PINEGROVE
PUBLISHING

PO Box 557 • Winona Lake, IN 46590

Also by John Davis,

Real Fishermen are Never Thin
(Paperback, 124 pages, $7.95)

Real Fishermen Never Lie
(Paperback, 124 pages, $7.95

Real Fishermen Never Wear Suits
(Paperback, 124 pages, $7.95)

Available from:

Pinegrove Publishing
P.O. Box 557
Winona Lake, IN 46590

Use the order blanks on pages 221 - 224 for ordering
the above books or additional copies of this recipe
book.

First Printing - Sept. 1995

ISBN 0-9635865-2-1

To

My wife, Carolyn, for her constant encouragement during this project,

and

My parents, John and Catherine, for making fishing a family affair.

TABLE OF CONTENTS

INTRODUCTION

Ever since I was knee-high to a nightcrawler, I have been around fish and fishermen. My boyhood days were spent along the coasts of south Jersey fishing for flounder, weakfish, blues, striped bass, and sea bass. My taste buds still tingle when I think of the marvelous seafood dinners I enjoyed at the many restaurants from Atlantic City to Cape May.

But my culinary interests were not only cultivated by the delights of seafood, but many trips to the beautiful Pocono Mountains of Pennsylvania where I was introduced to the joys of trout and smallmouth bass fishing.

Add to that my more than 35 years of living in north central Indiana with its hundreds of natural lakes which provide superb fishing, and you can easily see why I have this passion for fish and seafood.

I still enjoy hours on lakes, streams and rivers catching fish, but in recent years, I have taken particular pleasure in preparing and eating them.

This collection of recipes is the product of years of compiling materials, asking thousands of questions of good cooks and personal experience. I have attempted to include a wide range of recipes suitable for the beginning cook, the advanced gourmet chef and everybody in-between.

Fish and seafood have been popular table fares in the United States in recent years due largely to their health benefits. They are loaded with protein, B vitamins, phosphorus, iron, zinc, iodine and potassium. Since they are low in calories and saturated fat, they are the food of choice for those concerned about heart and arterial diseases.

Many fish are high in Omega-3 fatty acid which has proven beneficial to preventing heart attacks and strokes.

Improper care of your catch in the field or poor preparation in the kitchen can diminish many of these benefits, however. For that reason, we will begin our journey to good cooking with some attention to the matter of field care and the preservation of fish.

A wide array of seafood is now available at supermarkets across the country, but not all is top quality or fresh. We will provide some basic tips on how to buy fish and seafood so health problems can be prevented.

It is my hope that this modest collection of recipes will help spark new interest in eating some of the world's most beneficial foods. If a few smiles and enthusiastic compliments are produced at America's dinner tables as the result of using this book, the whole project will have been worthwhile.

ACKNOWLEDGMENTS

It is not possible to write and edit a recipe book with its hundreds of details without the assistance of many people. I want to acknowledge, with gratitude, their various contributions.

Special thanks is due to Kevin Carter for his usual mastery of graphics in designing the cover and the illustrations found throughout the book.

I wish to thank Sandy Kibbey for reading through the manuscript and making valuable suggestions.

Appreciation is expressed to Duane R. Lund for granting permission to reprint selected recipes from his two excellent books, <u>101 Favorite Freshwater Fish Recipes</u> and <u>Sauces, Seasonings and Marinades for Fish and Wild Game</u>. Information on the purchase of these books may be secured by writing him at P.O. Box 305, Staples, MI 56479.

To my friends and fellow compatriots in Hoosier Outdoor Writers Association, Jack Kerins and Jack Cooper, I express my gratitude for the recipes provided and for their encouragement in this project.

Many folks have shared their favorite fish and seafood recipes throughout the years and to them I am

9

most grateful. *Their contributions to this recipe collection are acknowledged at the appropriate places throughout the book.*

FIELD CARE OF FISH

The proper field care of fish or seafood will ultimately determine whether the evening meal will be enjoyed or merely endured.

Fish flesh is extremely perishable and requires careful preservation after the catch to insure its delicate flavors and texture. As a rule, the fatty fishes, whether freshwater or saltwater, will deteriorate more rapidly than leaner types (See the chart on page 210 for a listing of fat and lean fish).

Freshwater anglers should attempt to keep bluegills, perch, crappies and bass alive in livewells or live baskets. If the water in a boat livewell or basket is very warm and poor in oxygen, however, it is far better to ice the fish immediately in a cooler. This will reduce stress in the fish and guarantee a better taste. Fish that are still alive, but are in the process of dying are diminishing in quality.

To retain the best flavor, walleye, northerns and other large freshwater species should be placed in a cooler filled with crushed ice immediately after the catch. This is also true of all saltwater fish. It is a good idea to leave the cooler drain open so excesses water can drain out.

If stringers are employed, never put the snaps through the gills. Always put them through one or both lips of the fish. It is best to use nylon rather than metal stringers for muskies and northerns since they can twist metal snaps open.

If dry ice is available, it is excellent for either freezing fish or to keep them cool for long journeys. Dry ice is carbon dioxide in a sold state and has a temperature of minus 109° F. The one problem with using this in the field is that it is very heavy. A 10-inch block weighs 54 pounds!

A five pound fish can be frozen in ten minutes if wrapped in newspaper and placed between two one-inch slabs of dry ice.

Be sure to place the identity of frozen fish on the package and the date that it was frozen.

It is best to thaw frozen fish in a refrigerator, but good planning will be required to do this since it takes a great deal of time. Do not leave fish uncovered while thawing. If a fish has been glazed, wash off the ice coating with cold water, re-wrap the fish loosely and let it thaw in a refrigerator or at room temperature if immediate use is desired.

PRESERVING FISH

The really great fish dinners are those that are caught, cleaned and cooked the same day. But this is not always possible or practical so methods of storing fish must be employed.

Fresh fish should not be kept in the refrigerator more than two days. Long term storage of fish usually requires freezing. All fish should be cleaned before freezing and the quicker the freeze, the better.

Freezer temperatures that produce best results are those that fall between minus 10° F. to minus 15° F.

There are several freezing methods that work well for varying periods of time. The real enemy of good storage is the evaporation of moisture in the fish over time resulting in "freezer burn". This can be prevented by employing one of several different sealing methods depending on the anticipated storage time.

The block freezing method is one of the most popular and will preserve fish for up to a year. As the term suggests, fish are frozen in a block of ice. Panfish, for example, can be placed in a water-filled milk carton and frozen very effectively. Other wax or metal lined containers can be employed for the larger fish.

Vacuum packers are now readily available for home use and they do a superb job of preparing fish for long-term freezing. With all the air removed from the package, fish can be kept frozen for up to a year without damage.

Glazing a whole fish is an old, but proven, method of preserving fish. First freeze the fish hard then dip it in ice water until a coat of ice covers the entire fish. Make sure there are no exposed portions of the fish. It might be necessary to reinforce the glaze from time to time. The fish should be wrapped with as little air inside as possible.

Smoked fish should be refrigerated for best preservation. If such fish need to be frozen, they should be thawed slowly in a refrigerator.

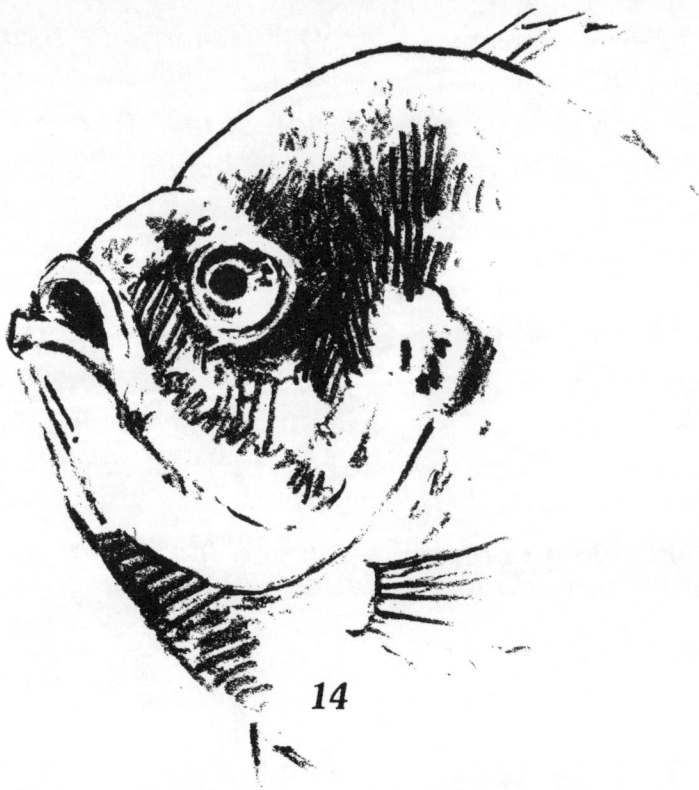

COOKING METHODS

Fish have very delicate flesh with little connective tissue which means they cook very rapidly. Cooking fish too long or at too high temperature will make them tough. Fish are usually finished when the flesh becomes opaque and flakes easily.

As in other animal flesh, texture and flavor are closely related. Handling fish properly from the catch to the kitchen will determine their palatability.

An excellent way to determine the cooking time of fish is to measure the diameter of the fish at its widest point, and allow 10 minutes cooking time for each inch or fraction thereof.

For example, if a salmon measured 2-inches at its widest point, the cooking time would be 20 minutes. This method is often called the Canadian Method of cooking and is widely used by chefs and outdoor people.

Baking should be done at 10 minutes for each inch in a 450° F. oven.

According to some chefs, this approach works just as well with frozen fish as it does with fresh. They suggest that the fish not be thawed, but cooked frozen with the time doubled per inch of diameter. For example, a two-inch diameter will be cooked for 40 minutes rather than the 20 for fresh fish. Deep frying frozen fish is not recommended.

Cooking methods fall into at least five categories: 1. <u>Deep-frying</u> (boiling the fish in oil or lard at 375° F.), 2. <u>Frying</u> (pan-frying, stir-frying and pan-frying), 3. <u>Dry Cooking</u> (baking, broiling, and oven-frying) 4. <u>Wet Cooking</u> (steaming, braising, poaching) and 5. <u>Microwave</u>.

The following are some of the basic methods of cooking fish:

<u>Deep Frying</u>: Fish are coated with a batter and dipped in oil heated to 375° F. Cooking time is usually about 10 minutes per inch at this temperature.

<u>Baking</u>: The oven should be pre-heated to between 425° F. and 450° F. The fish can be baked without wrapping or it may be wrapped in paper or foil for which an extra amount of time should be allowed in order that the heat might penetrate the covering.

<u>Broiling</u>: Before preheating the broiler, be sure to coat the surface where the fish will be placed with oil. The fish should positioned about three to four inches from the heat (Most broilers will produce heat at the 500° F. to 525° F. level). If the fish is frozen or dressed, place it five inches from the heat. Be sure to baste often with oil or butter.

16

Grilling: This method of cooking fish and seafood has gained great popularity in recent years and yields some great results. Fish should be placed on a well-oiled rack or piece of foil and positioned no closer than six inches from the flames. Basting frequently is important to prevent the fish from drying out.

Pan Frying: This method usually requires 1/4-inch of melted butter or oil in a pan. The fish is fried until golden brown on one side, then it is turned.

Oven Frying: Preheat the oven to 500° F. and placed breaded fish near the top of the oven on a lightly greased pan. Baste fish with butter or oil during the cooking time.

Poaching: Bring milk or water to a boil and place the fish in it. The timing is the same as with other methods---about 10 minutes per inch of thickness.

Braising: Begin by sautéing carrots, onions and a clove of garlic (cut in thin strips) in butter for about five minutes. Arrange them on the bottom of a frying pan then place the fish on top. Pour in red or white wine or a mixture of wine and fish bouillon until it covers one-half the fish. Once the liquid reaches a boil, allow 10 minutes cooking time per inch of thickness.

Steaming: Position fish on a plate or rack above boiling water. Place a lid over the pot or wok. Cooking time will follow the Canadian Method described above.

17

TIPS FOR BUYING FISH

Improperly stored fish or seafood can provide some surprises you don't really want. About 50% of our seafood now comes from abroad and many of the countries of origin do not maintain the same standards of handling that are current here in the United States.

Ciguatoxin, a tasteless and odorless toxin is a natural substance found in fish that feed on tropical reefs. While many fish contain this substance, large quantities in badly kept fish can pose serious heath risks. Scombroid poisoning can develop from tuna, mackerel, bluefish and mahi mahi that have not been properly chilled after being caught.

In the light of the above, it is important to know the store from which you purchase your fish or sea-food, and its buying policies.

The old saying about eating oysters in months with an "r" in them is good advice. Months so designated are the cold months and are not likely to produce the dangerous vibrio bacteria.

Here are some guidelines for purchasing fish or seafood from the market.

1. Avoid purchasing filets that are piled high with no ice around the sides or top.

18

2. The eyes of the fish should be bright, clear, and bulging. The gills should be bright red and the fish fresh-smelling (without strong odors).

3. There should be no discoloration.

4. The flesh should be firm and spring back when pressed.

5. Frozen fish should be solidly frozen when purchased. The appearance should be firm and glossy with no evidence of drying out. There should be no white spots or parched, paper-like corners or edges. The wrapping should be of moisture-vaporproof material with no air space between the wrapping and the fish.

The amount of fish you buy for each serving will vary in accordance the way the fish was prepared and stored. Generally speaking, fish in the round will require 1 lb. pan-dressed fish; 1/2 lb. fillets with bones removed, 1/4 lb.

****

Angler: A guy who, first of all, lies in wait for a fish then lies in weight after he lands it.

SAUCES, BUTTERS AND BATTERS

SAUCES AND BUTTERS

The "tour de force" of many fish and seafood dinners is in the sauces or butters used. Such accompaniments are especially critical when fish are baked or broiled. The following is a collection of sauces and butters that are suitable for use with fish or seafood.

SAUCES

For Basting

Butter Basting Sauce

1/2 cup butter, melted
1 tsp. garlic, minced
Salt, pepper, paprika, parsley- all sautéed.

Traditional Basting Sauce

1/2 cup mayonnaise
2 Tbsp. catsup
2 tsp. mustard
Salt, pepper and paprika.

All-Purpose Sauce

May be brushed on almost any variety of fish while broiling or baking. Season fish first, however, with salt and pepper. Ingredients for about 1 1/2 lbs. fillets:

1/8 lb. butter, melted (1/2 stick)
2 Tbsp. soy sauce
1 tsp. garlic powder
1 Tbsp. olive oil
2 Tbsp. lemon juice

1. Blend together all ingredients, keep warm and use to baste fish (every few minutes for broiling, every 10 minutes for baking).

Courtesy Duane R. Lund, <u>Sauces, Seasonings and Marinades for Fish and Wild Game</u>.

Spicy Basting Sauce

3/8 cup steak sauce
1/4 cup butter, melted
1 tsp. vinegar
1 tsp. catsup

Hot Basting Sauce

Use for basting and serve the balance of the sauce over grilled or baked salmon or trout.
Ingredients for 3 lbs. steak or 6 lbs. whole salmon.

1 Tbsp. butter, melted
1 cup fish stock*
1 small onion, chopped
2 Tbsp. garlic, minced
1 can Italian style tomatoes
1 small green or red pepper, chopped
1 Tbsp. basil or other favorite herb, chopped
1 Tbsp. parsley, chopped
4 drops Tabasco sauce

*See page 114

Sauté the onion and garlic in the butter. Add all other ingredients. Stir and cook over low heat until about 1/3 of the liquid has evaporated.

Courtesy Duane R. Lund, Sauces, Seasonings and Marinades for Fish and Wild Game

****

A fisherman is a guy who catches a big fish by patience, and sometimes by luck, but most often by the ...tale.

Spicy Broiling Sauce

Spoon this sauce on the fish while it is broiling. Left-over sauce may be served with the fish. This recipe came from Texas. Ingredients for about 2 lbs. of fillets or steaks.

2 Tbsp. onion, chopped
1 tsp. garlic, minced
3/4 cup chili sauce
2 Tbsp. Worcestershire sauce
3 Tbsp. brown sugar
1/2 tsp. chili powder
2 Tbsp. lemon juice
Dash of salt
Enough butter to sauté onion and garlic

1. Sauté the onion and garlic until the onion is clear; be careful not to burn.

2. Add all other ingredients.

3. Let simmer over low heat for 10 minutes, stirring regularly to blend thoroughly.

Courtesy Duane R. Lund, <u>Sauces, Seasonings, and Marinades for Fish and Wild Game</u>.

****

There are more fish taken out of a lake than were ever in it.

Oriental Sauce

1/4 cup orange juice
2 Tbsp. soy sauce
2 Tbsp. catsup
2 Tbsp. lemon juice
1/2 tsp. oregano
1/2 tsp. pepper
2 Tbsp. parsley, chopped
1 clove garlic, minced

Lemon Sauce

Juice of 1 lemon
1/2 tsp. garlic salt
1/4 cup melted butter
1/4 tsp. pepper

Wine Sauce

1/4 cup olive oil
1 tsp. rosemary
1/2 cup tomato, diced
1 Tbsp. lemon juice
1 cup dry white wine
Salt and pepper to taste

Barbecue Sauce

For salmon steaks or fillets.

1 cup butter, melted
1/3 cup lemon juice
1 1/2 tsp. soy sauce
1 1/2 tsp. Worcestershire sauce
2 Tbsp. fresh parsley
1 tsp. sweet basil
1 tsp. oregano
1/2 tsp. garlic powder
Salt and pepper to taste

1. Combine all sauce ingredients.

2. Place fish on a grill or in a broiler and brush with sauce.

3. Broil equally on each side and brush on additional sauce before each turn.

Creamy Dill Sauce

This sauce works well with just about any freshwater or saltwater fish. Ingredients for about 1 1/2 lbs. of fillets.

1 cup half and half or whole milk
1 tsp. fresh dill, chopped
1 tsp. chives, chopped
Salt and pepper to taste

1. Use a baking dish and place a single layer of fillets on the bottom of the dish.

2. Season lightly with salt and pepper. Add the half and half (or milk); stop adding when the liquid begins to cover the fish.

3. Sprinkle the chopped dill and chives on the fillets. Spoon a little of the liquid on the fillets.

4. Bake in a medium oven until the fish flakes easily.

5. The time will depend on the amount of fish and liquid, but begin checking after about 30 minutes.

6. Spoon the milk or cream over the fillets about every 10 minutes.

Courtesy Duane R. Lund, <u>Sauces, Seasonings and Marinades for Fish and Wild Game</u>.

General Application Sauces

Cocktail Sauce Lamaze

1 cup mayonnaise
1 cup chili sauce
1/4 cup Indian relish
1/2 hard boiled egg, chopped
1/2 tsp. chives, chopped
1/4 green pepper, chopped
1/2 pimento, chopped
1/2 Tbsp. celery, chopped
1/2 Tbsp. prepared mustard
1 dash paprika
1/2 Tbsp. A-1 Sauce.

1. Mix all ingredients and serve with any seafood.

****

A Texan was telling about some of the fish in the pond back home. He'd taken a picture of one of the smaller ones, and the picture weighed five pounds.

Egg Sauce

1 Tbsp. butter
1 Tbsp. flour
1 cup hot fish stock*
1 egg yolk

* See page 114

1.   Melt butter and add flour. Mix well.

2.   Add hot fish stock gradually and boil 1 minute
     stirring constantly.

3.   Remove from heat and pour gradually over beaten
     egg yolk.

4.   Pour while hot over boiled fish and garnish with
     parsley.

White Clam Sauce

1 dozen clams, chopped
1/4 cup olive oil
1 clove garlic, sliced
1 Tbsp. onion, chopped
1/2 cup clam juice
Cooked spaghetti
Mint leaves

1. Cook onions and garlic in olive oil until golden.

2. Add clams and juice.

3. Cover and heat 5 minutes.

4. Pour over spaghetti and top with mint leaves.

Tartar Sauce - A

1 cup mayonnaise
3 Tbsp. dill pickle, finely chopped
1 Tbsp. onion, finely chopped
1 tsp. parsley, finely chopped
1 tsp. sugar

Tartar Sauce - B

1 cup mayonnaise
2 Tbsp. capers, finely chopped
2 Tbsp. olives, finely chopped
2 Tbsp. gherkins, finely chopped
1 Tbsp. parsley, finely chopped
1/4 tsp. of onion juice or shallots, finely chopped

****

Tartar Sauce - C

1 cup mayonnaise or salad dressing
1 1/2 Tbsp. sour pickles, chopped
1 1/2 Tbsp. olives, chopped
1 Tbsp. onion, grated
1 Tbsp. parsley, chopped

Tartar Sauce - D

1 cup mayonnaise
2 dill pickles, grated
1/2 medium onion, grated
1/8 head cabbage, grated

Cranberry Tartar Sauce

1 cup mayonnaise or salad dressing
1/2 cup jellied cranberry sauce
2 Tbsp. onion, chopped
1/4 cup sweet pickle relish
2 Tbsp. olives, chopped (optional)
2 Tbsp. parsley, chopped

****

Lemon Tartar Sauce

1/2 cup mayonnaise or salad dressing
2 Tbsp. dill pickle, finely chopped
2 Tbsp. green onion, finely chopped
1 Tbsp. canned pimento, chopped (optional)
1 tsp. fresh lemon peel, grated
2 tsp. lemon juice, freshly squeezed

Tomato and Cheese Sauce

1 onion, minced
1/2 green pepper, minced
3 Tbsp. butter or olive oil
1 1/3 cups canned tomato purée
1/2 tsp. fennel
1/2 cup sharp cheese, grated
Salt and pepper

1. Sauté the onion and green pepper in butter or oil for 3 minutes.

2. Add the salt, pepper and purée and simmer again for 10 minutes.

3. Add fennel and cheese and sir until the cheese is melted. Take off the heat immediately.

Herbed Sauce

1/4 cup sweet pickle, finely chopped
2 1/2 Tbsp. green onion, finely chopped
1 Tbsp. parsley, minced
1/2 clove garlic, minced
2 cups mayonnaise
1 tsp. dry mustard
1 tsp. paprika
1/2 tsp. salt
Dash pepper

1. Mix pickle, onion, parsley and garlic.

2. Put in fine sieve and press to extract as much juice as possible.

3. Add juice to mayonnaise. Stir in remaining ingredients.

Halibut Sauce

2 cups ketchup
1 1/2 - 2 tsp. horseradish

1. Mix and let set at least an hour before serving.

Indian Curry Sauce

1/4 cup butter
1/4 cup onion, chopped
2 1/2 Tbsp. flour
1/2 to 2 tsp. curry powder
A pinch to 1/4 tsp. saffron (optional)
1 cup chicken broth
1/2 tsp. lemon peel, grated

1. Sauté butter and onion slowly until tender.

2. Stir in and cook, for 4 to 5 minutes: flour, curry powder and saffron.

3. Add slowly, stirring constantly, and simmer until well blended: chicken broth, cream and grated lemon peel. If you wish to have a perfectly smooth sauce, add the chicken broth and grated lemon peel only.

4. Cook 10 minutes, strain through sieve, add the cream and bring back to boil.

****

Fishing: Eternal optimism and never-ending disappointment

Cream and Onion Sauce

1 lb. white onions, sliced
1/2 cup butter
1 cup thick cream sauce*
Dash nutmeg or mace
1/4 cup cream

*Thick cream sauce:

2 Tbsp. butter
4 Tbsp. flour
1 cup cream
Salt and pepper

1. Make the thick cream sauce by melting the butter in a saucepan and mixing in the flour
   and gradually adding the cream to make a
   smooth paste. Heat slowly and cook until very
   thick. Put aside.

2. Cook the onions in the butter and when
   they are soft mash through a sieve.
   Add these to the thick cream sauce.

3. Season and serve over boiled or broiled fish.

Dill Sauce

2 Tbsp. green onion, finely chopped
2 Tbsp. parsley, finely chopped
1 Tbsp. fresh dill, finely chopped
  (or 1 tsp. dried dillweed)
Salt and pepper to taste
2/3 cup mayonnaise
2/3 cup sour cream

1. Mix together mayonnaise and sour cream. Add remaining ingredients.

Snappy Cocktail Sauce

1/2 cup catsup
1 heaping Tbsp. prepared horseradish
3 Tbsp. sugar
1 Tbsp. A-1 sauce
1 1/2 tsp. lemon juice
1/2 tsp. Worcestershire sauce
8 drops Tabasco sauce
Salt and pepper (fresh ground) to taste

1. Combine all ingredients in a small bowl and mix well.

Sweet and Sour Sauce

1 cup ketchup
2 cups sugar
1 cup vinegar
Juice of 1/2 lemon
1 Tbsp. soy sauce

1. Mix well in a saucepan, bring to boil.

2. Then combine: 1 cup water and 1 Tbsp. corn
   starch. Thicken with corn starch and serve warm.

Asparagus Sauce

Serve hot over fillets or steaks.
Ingredients for about 2 lbs. fillets.

1 lb. asparagus, fresh
1 cup cream
1 egg
Salt and pepper to taste

1. Cut asparagus into 1/2-inch chunks. Cook in
   boiling water until tender. Drain.

2. Put asparagus, cream and egg in blender
   and blend until smooth. Add salt and pepper
   to taste. Heat in saucepan and serve over
   the fillets or steaks.

Courtesy Duane R. Lund, <u>Sauces, Seasonings and Marinades for Fish and Wild Game</u>.

Mustard Dill Sauce

1 cup mustard sauce
1 Tbsp. hot, Dijon-style prepared mustard
2 Tbsp. fresh dill, minced

1. Mix the mustard sauce and Dijon well.

2. Add the minced fresh dill.

3. Serve with smoked fish.

****

It has been observed that if fishermen talked only about the fish they really caught, the silence would be unbearable.

Cooper's Army Sauce

"The best seafood sauce/dip I've come across is a simple one given to me by my army cooking school instructor more than 40 years ago. The ingredients can be varied according to your tastes and at our house it's also a favorite as a poultry dip."

Jack Cooper, Indianapolis, Indiana

1 cup prepared mustard
1 cup barbecue sauce
1 cup Miracle Whip
1 cup strained honey
2 Tbsp. horseradish, minced (can substitute 3 Tbsp. horseradish sauce)
2 tsp. creme of tartar
Dash lemon juice
Dash Tabasco sauce

1. To vary taste and texture mix in 2 Tbsp. sweet relish or 2 Tbsp. chili powder or use "smoke flavored" barbecue sauce.

2. Mix all ingredients thoroughly. Keep refrigerated in closed container. Stir slightly before serving.

This mixture can be used to coat before baking/broiling fish etc., served chilled or at room temperature as a dip, or heated and served over or beside as a sauce for the entree.

Spinach Sauce

Use over sautéed fish fillets

2 lbs. fresh spinach
1/4 lb. butter (1 stick)
1 large onion, finely chopped
1 Tbsp. garlic, minced
4 Tbsp. lemon juice
Salt and pepper

1. Cut or tear spinach into quite small pieces.

2. Melt about 1/3 of the butter and sauté the spinach, onion and garlic in a pan until tender. The spinach will take on a wilted look when done.

3. Stir in the lemon juice. Sprinkle on a little freshly ground pepper.

4. Meanwhile, sauté the fillets in the remainder of the butter.

5. Remove the fillets and pour any remaining butter over the spinach. Spoon the spinach mixture over the fish and serve.

Courtesy Duane R. Lund, <u>Sauces, Seasonings and Marinades for Fish and Wild Game.</u>

Creamy Mustard Sauce

Serve over broiled or poached fish.

1 1/2 cups of cream
4 Tbsp. mustard
3/4 cup onion or chives, finely chopped
Salt and pepper
Optional: white wine (1/2 cup)

1. If you use chopped onion, sauté for 3 to 4 minutes in butter until the onion is clear. If you use chives, they need not be sautéed. You may choose to use a mix of onion and chives.

2. If you wish to use wine, add about 1/2 cup to the onions and heat until nearly all of it has evaporated; stir occasionally so that the onions do not burn.

Courtesy Duane R. Lund, <u>Sauces, Seasonings and Marinades for Fish and Wild Game</u>.

43

Spicy Dipping Sauce

A good sauce for dipping pieces of broiled, poached or baked fish.

1 cup fish stock*
2 Tbsp. soy sauce
2 Tbsp. Worcestershire sauce
2 Tbsp. sherry
2 Tbsp. butter, melted
*See page 114

1. Blend, heat and serve hot.

Courtesy Duane R. Lund, <u>Sauces, Seasonings and Marinades for Fish and Wild Game</u>.

Almond Sauce

1/2 cup butter
1/2 cup almonds, slivered
1 Tbsp. lemon juice
2 Tbsp. white cooking wine
1/4 tsp. salt
Dash of black pepper

1. Melt butter in a small saucepan. Add almonds and sauté over low heat to a golden brown color.

2. Add remaining ingredients and shake pan over heat for 2 minutes.

Creamy Cocktail Sauce

1 cup mayonnaise
1 1/4 cup chili sauce
1 1/4 cup prepared horseradish
1 tsp. lemon juice
1 1/4 tsp. Worcestershire sauce

Tarragon Cream Sauce

Ingredients for 2 lbs. fish fillets or steaks:

1 Tbsp. fresh tarragon, minced
1 cup fish stock*
1 cup heavy cream
1 cup white wine

*See page 114

1. Combine tarragon, fish stock and wine in a sauce pan and bring to a boil.

2. Continue heating and stirring until only about 2/3 of a cup of liquid remains.

3. Lower heat, add cream, continue stirring over low heat until sauce thickens.

Courtesy Duane R. Lund, Sauces, Seasonings and Marinades for Fish and Wild Game.

Lemon-Herb Sauce

A basting sauce for baked or broiled fish.

Ingredients for 1 1/2 lbs. fillets or steaks, or 3 lbs. whole fish.

1/4 lb. butter, melted
2 Tbsp. lemon juice
2 Tbsp. parsley, chopped
2 Tbsp. chives, chopped
1 Tbsp. thyme or other favorite herb
Salt and pepper to taste

1. Stir together all ingredients. Brush on the fish two or three times while baking or broiling.

Courtesy Duane R. Lund, <u>Sauces, Seasonings and Marinades for Fish and Wild Game</u>.

Dill Sauce

Ingredients for approximately 4 lbs. fillets or a 6 lb. baked fish (live weight).

2 Tbsp. fresh dill, minced or 1 Tbsp. dry dill
1 Tbsp. onion, chopped
2 Tbsp. butter

1 Tbsp. flour
1/2 cup cream
1 cup fish stock*
Salt and pepper to taste

*See page 114

1. Sauté the onion pieces until clear.

2. Stir in flour and cook for 3 minutes.

3. Stir in all other ingredients, seasoning to taste.

4. Serve hot over fillets, steaks or baked fish.

Courtesy Duane R. Lund, <u>Sauces, Seasonings and Marinades for Fish and Wild Game</u>.

Shrimp Sauce

1 1/2 cups olive oil
1/2 cup vinegar
1 tsp. onion juice
Powdered mustard (to personal taste)
1 or 2 cloves of garlic
Few drops of hot sauce
Salt, pepper and paprika to taste

1. Make 2 or 3 days ahead of time. Shake well before using.

Alaskan Barbecue Sauce

May be used on fillets or whole fish while they are broiling or when the fish is served. Designed for salmon, but works very well with lake trout or northern pike. It also works miracles for catfish or bullheads!

Ingredients for 2 lbs. of fillets or steaks:

1/2 lb. butter
1 clove garlic, diced
4 Tbsp. soy sauce
2 Tbsp. mustard
1/4 cup catsup
Dash Worcestershire sauce

1. Using a double boiler, melt the butter.

2. Stir in all the other ingredients and continue heating for about 20 minutes, stirring occasionally.

3. Brush part of the liquid on the fillets or steaks while they are broiling and serve the balance (hot) with the meal.

Courtesy Mary Hayenga, St. Cloud, Mn. From *Sauces, Seasonings and Marinades for Fish and Wild Game* by Duane R. Lund.

Cucumber Sauce - A

1/2 cup Kraft Real Mayonnaise
1/2 cup dairy sour cream
1/2 cup cucumber, finely chopped
2 Tbsp. onion, chopped
1/2 tsp. dill weed

1. Mix all ingredients well.

Cucumber Sauce- B

1 medium cucumber (skin on), grated
2 Tbsp. onion, chopped very fine
2 Tbsp. vinegar
1 Tbsp. lettuce or parsley, chopped
1 1/4 cups mayonnaise
1 1/2 cups sour cream
Salt and pepper

1. Remove seeds from cucumber and grate. Blend all ingredients well then refrigerate.

****

There was this fellow in Wisconsin who caught a giant muskie. The poor guy dislocated both shoulders describing it.

Baked Fish Sauce

1 cup medium white sauce
2 tsp. Worcestershire sauce
1 tsp. prepared mustard
1 Tbsp. capers
1 cup cheddar cheese, grated
1 tsp. paprika
1 cup beer

1. Combine white sauce, cheese, Worcestershire sauce, paprika and mustard

2. Stir over low heat until cheese melts.

3. Add beer slowly while stirring.

4. Add capers. Serve hot.

White Sauce

2 Tbsp. butter
2 Tbsp. flour
1 cup milk
1/2 tsp. salt
Dash of pepper

1. Melt butter, remove from heat.

2. Add flour and mix until smooth.

3. Add milk and cook until thick, stirring constantly, to avoid lumps. Season.

Tangy Sauce

1 Tbsp. flour
1/2 tsp. salt
1 Tbsp. butter or margarine
1/4 tsp. paprika
3/4 cup milk
1 Tbsp. sweet pickle, chopped
1 hard cooked egg, chopped
1 Tbsp. lemon juice

1. Melt butter, add flour, salt and paprika.

2. Stir over a low flame until smooth.

3. Add milk slowly, stirring constantly until mixture thickens and boils.

4. Stir in rest of ingredients.

5. Serve hot.

****

Mushroom Sauce

1/3 cup onion, sliced
2 Tbsp. butter or margarine
1 cup milk
1/4 tsp. dried thyme (optional)
1 can condensed cream-of-mushroom soup (undiluted)
1/4 tsp. salt

1. In saucepan, sauté the onions in butter until they are tender and golden.

2. Gradually stir in the soup, then milk.

3. Add seasonings, heat, stirring constantly.

Tomato Sauce

1 onion, diced
2 Tbsp. butter
2 Tbsp. flour
1 1/2 cups canned tomato juice
1/2 tsp. salt
Dash of pepper

1. Sauté onion in butter until tender.

2. Mix in flour and brown until light golden color.

3. Add the tomato juice and seasonings, stirring constantly.

4. Boil on low heat for 3 or 4 minutes.

5. Serve hot.

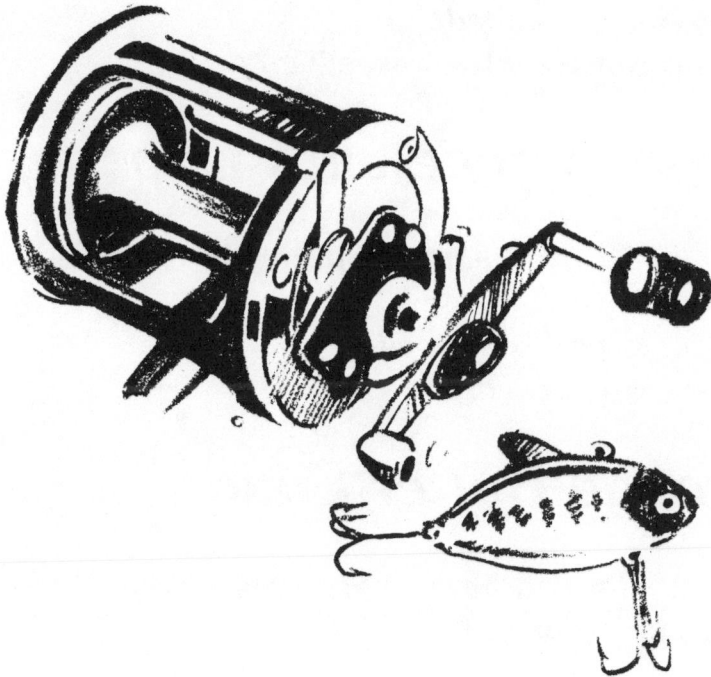

FLAVORED BUTTERS

Seasoned Butter

1 cup butter, melted
1 tsp. salt
1/2 tsp. pepper

Almond Butter

1 cup butter, melted
1/2 cup toasted almonds, slivered

Butter Sauce with Capers

1 cup of butter, heated (until it froths and begins to
   brown)
1 Tbsp. capers, chopped
1 tsp. cider vinegar

Orange Butter Sauce

6 Tbsp. clarified butter (See p. 55, Note 2)
1 1/2 cups orange juice

1. Let orange juice simmer over a low-medium heat
    until volume is reduced by one-half. Stir in liquid
    butter.

Fish Stock and Butter Sauce

1 cup fish stock[1]
1/4 cup clarified butter[2]
2 Tbsp. flour
1/2 tsp. salt
1/2 tsp. lemon juice

1. Blend flour into melted butter.

2. Gradually blend in fish stock.

3. Heat in saucepan until sauce bubbles and begins to thicken.

4. Remove from heat, add lemon juice and salt to taste.

[1] See page 114.

[2] *Clarified butter:* Melt butter and let cool until solids settle out to the bottom. Skim off the clear liquid on the top.

Courtesy Duane R. Lund, *Sauces, Seasonings and Marinades for Fish and Wild Game*.

****

Some of the best fishermen got married because a woman bit on their line.

Green Mayonnaise

2 cups Mayonnaise
2 Tbsp. parsley, chopped
1 Tbsp. tarragon leaves
1 Tbsp. chives, chopped
1 tsp. chervil, chopped
1 tsp. dill, chopped

Seafood Salad Dressing

2 cups mayonnaise
1 1/2 cups chili sauce
1/4 cup sour pickles, chopped
1/4 cup celery, chopped
1 tsp. lemon juice
1 tsp. horseradish
1/2 tsp. Worcestershire sauce

BATTERS

Bass Batter - A

2 cups flour
1 1/2 tsp. salt
1 1/2 tsp. baking powder
2/3 cup oil

1. Mix ingredients well.

2. Add water to thin to desired consistency.

3. Serve with sweet-and-sour sauce.

Bass Batter - B

1 cup Bisquick
1/2 cup milk
1 egg
Salt and pepper to taste

1. Beat milk and eggs.

2. Dip fish in mixture.

3. Roll in Bisquick which has been mixed with salt
    and pepper.

Bass Batter - C

2/3 cup corn starch
2/3 cup corn meal
1/3 cup flour
2 tsp. salt
4 tsp. baking powder

1. Mix all ingredients and add water slowly until
    desired texture is reached.

Shrimp Batter

2 eggs
1 cup milk
1 cup flour
1 tsp. salt
1 tsp. baking powder
Clove garlic or liquid garlic juice (to taste)

****

I never lost a little fish---
Yes, I am free to say.
It always was the biggest fish
I caught, that got away.

Eugene Field

Smelt Batter

1 cup buttermilk pancake mix
1/2 cup instant mashed potatoes
2 Tbsp. oil
2 Tbsp. parsley flakes
2 Tbsp. onion, minced and dried
1 tsp. salt
1/2 tsp. pepper
Beer

1. Mix all dry ingredients.

2. Add oil and beer to mixture to make batter like heavy syrup. Let stand 1 hour.

3. Before dipping, add more beer until batter is at syrup stage again.

Bluegill Batter - A

1/3 cup white flour
1/3 cup pancake flour
2 eggs
Salt & pepper (to taste)
Stale beer

1. Mix ingredients thoroughly.

2. Add stale beer to mixture until proper consistency
    is reached.

Bluegill Batter - B

2 eggs beaten
2 tsp. French's Yellow Mustard
Mashed potato flakes

1. Dip bluegills in egg-mustard mixture.

2. Then dip in mashed potato flakes.

3. Deep fry or pan fry until meat flakes.

****

Tempura Batter

1 cup flour
1 cup buttermilk
1/2 tsp. baking soda
1 egg
1/2 tsp. salt

Can be used with fish or seafood.

Oriental Batter

1 cup flour
1 cup cornstarch
3 Tbsp. baking powder
3 eggs

1. Mix dry ingredients with water until proper consistency is reached.

2. Add the 3 eggs and mix well.

****

Smelt: A highly edible fish, truly delicious, that should go to court and get its name changed.

Catfish Batter

3 egg yolks
3/4 cup water
1/3 cup cornstarch
1/2 cup flour
1/4 tsp. salt

1. Stir egg yolks to mix (don't beat).

2. Stir in water.

3. Combine cornstarch, salt, and flour; mix into liquid and stir lightly.

Lemon Batter

1 egg
3/4 cup water
Juice of 1 lemon
1 cup flour
1 tsp. baking powder
1 tsp. salt

1. Beat egg until light.

2. Add water and lemon juice.

3. Sift the flour, salt and baking powder into a bowl; stir in egg mixture lightly, until smooth.

Perch Batter

2 eggs
1 cup milk
1 1/2 cups all-purpose flour
1 Tbsp. baking powder
1 tsp. salt

1. Sift dry ingredients into a mixing bowl.

2. Beat eggs and mix in milk.

3. Make a well in the flour, pour in the liquid, and mix, working from the middle.

Crisp Crappie Batter

1 cup all-purpose flour
2 tsp. baking powder
1 1/2 tsp. salt
1 tsp. sugar
1 Tbsp. salad oil
1 cup water

1. Mix and sift dry ingredients into a bowl and make a well in the middle.

2. Mix oil and water and pour into the well while stirring mixture from the middle outward.

Walleye Batter

1 cup flour
1 tsp. baking powder
1 1/2 tsp. sugar
1 cup milk
1 egg
1 tsp. salt

1. Mix all ingredients thoroughly.

Beer Batter - A

2 egg whites
2 Tbsp. oil
1/3 cup beer
3/4 cup Bisquick
Garlic salt
Pepper
Salt

1. Beat egg whites until fluffy.

2. Add remaining ingredients.

****

It got so dry in northern Indiana, back in the 30's, that there were bass three years old that had never learned to swim.

64

Beer Batter - B

1 egg, beaten
1 tsp. salt
1 tsp. sugar
1 tsp. baking powder
1 cup flour
1 cup beer (room temperature)

1. Mix all ingredients well.

Beer Batter - C

1 can light beer
1 cup all-purpose flour
1 Tbsp. salt
1 Tbsp. pepper

1. Pour beer into a bowl.

2. Mix and sift dry ingredients into the beer, stirring with a whisk until batter is light and frothy.

****

An octopus is a fish built like a government agency.

Beer Batter - D

1 cup Bisquick
1/2 tsp. salt
1 egg
1 cup beer

1. Combine all ingredients then coat fish lightly.

Kentucky Batter

1 egg, beaten
3/4 cup cornmeal
1/2 cup Kentucky Colonel seasoned flour

1. Mix cornmeal and seasoned flour.

2. Dip fish fillets into egg.

3. Coat fish with cornmeal and seasoned flour.

****

FRESHWATER FISH

Barbecued Bass

4 bass fillets, 6-8 ounces each
4 lemon or lime slices
4 Tbsp. green onion tops, finely chopped
6 Tbsp. butter
2 Tbsp. lemon or lime juice
1 Tbsp. garlic, minced
1/2 tsp. salt
1/4 tsp. dried mustard
1 Tbsp. parsley, chopped

This recipe can be prepared outdoors on a grill or inside.

1. Place bass fillets on individual sheets of heavy foil large enough to accommodate folding.

2. Center a lemon or lime slice on each fillet, and sprinkle with green onion.

3. Melt butter---with remaining ingredients---in a saucepan over a low heat. Mix thoroughly while heating.

4. Then, drizzle this mixture over each fillet.

5. Fold the foil and seal tight. Place each packet on the grill rack about 8-inches from the coals. Or, in a 350° F. oven, heat for 20 minutes.

Barbecued Silver Bass

2 lbs. silver bass fillets
1/2 cup cooking oil
1 tsp. salt
Dash pepper
1 clove garlic, minced
1 cup cheddar cheese, shredded
1 cup cracker crumbs.
1 cup barbecue sauce

1. Combine oil, salt, pepper and garlic.

2. Mix cheese and crumbs.

3. Dip each piece of fish into oil, drain, and roll in cheese-crumb mixture.

4. Arrange fish in a well greased baking dish.

5. Bake at 450° F. for 7 to 10 minutes.

6. Heat barbecue sauce. Spoon 1/2 of sauce over fish and keep remainder hot. Bake fish an additional 5 minutes or until it flakes easily with a fork.

****

Webster Lake Bass Stew

1 lb. bass fillets, cut into 1-inch chunks
1/2 cup onion, chopped
2 Tbsp. cooking oil
2 cans (10 3/4-oz. each) cream of potato soup
2 cups milk
1 can (1 lb.) tomato wedges, undrained
1 package (10-oz.) frozen mixed vegetables,
    thawed
1 can (8-oz.) whole kernel corn, drained
1 tsp. salt
1/8 tsp. pepper
1 small bay leaf

1. Cook onion in oil until tender, but not brown.

2. Add soup, milk, tomato wedges, vegetables, corn,
    salt, pepper and bay leaf; heat stirring occasionally
    until simmering.

3. Add fish and simmer approximately ten minutes
    or until fish flakes easily when tested with a fork.

****

71

Buttermilk Bass

Buttermilk
Self-rising flour
Salt
Pepper
Wesson Oil

1. Soak fish 30 minutes in buttermilk.

2. Season flour well with salt and pepper.

3. Dip fish in seasoned flour and fry a few at a time.

Mustard Grilled Bass

1/4 cup mustard
1 tsp. sugar
1 1/2 to 2 lbs. bass fillets
Sliced bacon
1/4 cup oil
1/2 tsp. salt

1. Combine mustard, oil, sugar, salt and pepper.

2. Wrap bacon around fish and fasten with food picks.

3. Brush with mustard sauce.

4. Grill 5 to 10 minutes.

5. Turn, brush with sauce and grill 5 to 10 minutes longer.

Bass Fillets

1 to 1 1/2 lbs. bass fillets
1 onion, sliced
Garlic powder
Salt
Pepper
Butter

1. Place bass fillets on large pieces of aluminum foil.

2. Salt and pepper to taste.

3. Add several pats of butter and sprinkle with garlic powder.

4. Add slices of onion to each package.

5. Seal and puncture ventilation holes in top.

6. Either bake in 350° F. oven for 1 hour or place on charcoal grill for 45 minutes to 1 hour.

Sesame Broiled Bass

1 1/2 lbs. bass fillets
1/2 cup butter, melted
1 Tbsp. lemon juice
1/2 tsp. dill weed
1 Tbsp. sesame seeds

1. Place fillets on a lightly greased broiler pan.

2. Baste fish with a mixture of lemon juice, melted butter and dill weed.

3. Place the broiler pan about 4-inches from the heat source and broil for about 3 or 4 minutes on the first side.

4. Turn the fillets and broil for an additional two or three minutes, then remove and sprinkle lightly with sesame seeds.

5. Return to the broiler for about one minute.

****

Achish Featherbelt is not much of a fisherman. Just last week he asked what kind of bait he should use to catch fishsticks.

Spicy Bass

1 lb. bass fillets
2 Tbsp. oil
1/2 tsp. hot pepper sauce
1/8 tsp. cayenne pepper
1/2 tsp. thyme
1/2 tsp. oregano
1/2 cup Italian style bread crumbs

1. In a small bowl, combine oil and hot pepper sauce, set aside.

2. On a shallow dish or platter, combine bread crumbs, cayenne pepper, thyme and oregano.

3. Lightly brush both sides of fish with oil mixture and then dip into bread crumb mixture.

4. Place fillets on a broiler pan. Broil 4-to 5-inches from heat for 10 minutes or until done.

****

An answer to this question
Is what I greatly wish
Does fishing make men liars---
Or do only liars fish?

Cedar Lodge Baked Fish

3 hamburger rolls, broken into small pieces
2 sprigs of parsley, chopped
2 Tbsp. oil
2 Tbsp. cheese, grated
1 garlic clove, finely chopped
1/2 tsp. oregano
1/2 green pepper, chopped
1 to 1 1/2 lbs. bass fillets
8-ounce can tomato sauce

1. Combine first 7 ingredients in a bowl.

2. Place fish fillets in a 9" by 13" baking dish.

3. Top with bread mixture.

4. Pour tomato sauce on top.

5. Sprinkle with oregano and about 2 Tbsp. of oil.

6. Bake in a 400° F. oven for 20 to 25 minutes.

****

Bluegill Soup

15 bluegills
1 1/2 qt. water
1/2 qt. tomato juice
1 Tbsp. basil leaves
Pinch thyme
1/2 cup celery, chopped
1/2 cup barley,
1 can okra (optional)
1 onion, chopped
2 Tbsp. parsley
Salt and pepper

1. Boil bluegills, water, tomato juice and salt and pepper slowly for 30 minutes.

2. Remove fish from the bones and set aside.

3. Add celery, barley, onion, basil, thyme and boil until celery is tender.

4. Add parsley, okra and bluegill meat and simmer 10 minutes.

Courtesy Walt Such, Westvill, Illinois

****

Broiled Bluegill

10 bluegills
Italian salad dressing
Lemon juice
Salt
Butter

1. Cover bottom of a baking dish with melted butter and place bluegills side by side.

2. Squeeze lemon juice over each fish.

3. Baste liberally with Italian salad dressing.

4. Broil until top side turns brown, turn and brown other side.

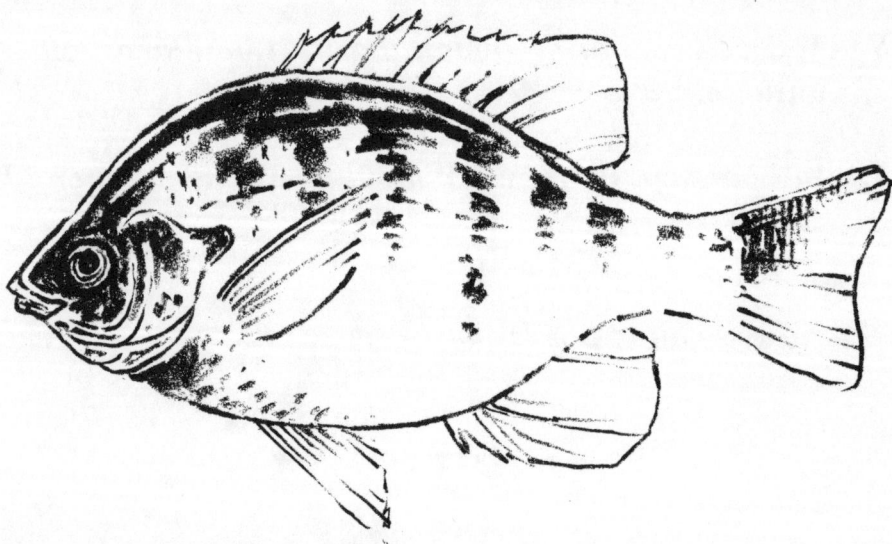

Buckeye Fried Bluegill

8 to 10 bluegills
2/3 cup cornmeal
1 Tbsp. lemon pepper seasoning
1 tsp. seasoned salt
1 egg, beaten
1/4 cup milk or water

1. Combine cornmeal, lemon pepper and seasoned salt on a sheet of aluminum foil.

2. Combine egg and milk in shallow dish or pie pan.

3. Dip fish in egg mixture.

4. Coat with cornmeal mixture.

5. Deep fry or pan fry in vegetable oil.

****

Fishermen's motto: Don't hurry...settle back...then bait and see.

Baked Sunfish

Sunfish fillets
1/2 stick butter
Lawry's seasoning salt and pepper
1 egg, well beaten
Italian seasoned bread crumbs

1. Melt butter in baking dish in 375° F. oven.

2. Dip seasoned fish in egg and seasoned bread crumbs.

3. Cook in baking dish for 20 to 25 minutes or until fish flakes with fork.

Bacon Fried Bluegills

8 - 10 bluegills
Bacon drippings
Salt and pepper
Flour

1. Mix salt, pepper and flour.

2. Coat fish well on both sides.

3. Heat 1/2-inch bacon drippings in skillet.

4. Place fish into hot bacon fat and fry for approximately 3 to 5 minutes each side.

5. Drain on paper towel before serving.

Bluegill Snacks

Bluegill fillets cut into bite-size pieces
1 cup flour
1 tsp. lemon peel, grated
1/2 tsp. salt
1/2 tsp. parsley flakes
1/4 tsp. pepper

1. Mix the dry ingredients.

2. Add 1 Tbsp. lemon juice and enough club soda to make a smooth batter.

3. Deep fry or pan fry until golden.

4. Serve with sweet-and-sour sauce or mustard sauce.

Panfish Snacks

1 lb. panfish filets
1/2 cup flour
1 tsp. salt
1/2 tsp. garlic powder
1/4 tsp. paprika
Cocktail sauce

1. Mix dry ingredients.

2. Coat the fillets well.

3. Deep fry until crisp.

4. Serve with cocktail sauce or sweet-and-sour sauce.

Delicious Bluegill Fillets

8 - 10 bluegill fillets
Ritz crackers, crushed
Creamy French dressing
Cheddar cheese, grated

1. Roll fillets in crackers.

2. Dip in French dressing.

3. Roll in cheese.

4. Place in a greased baking dish.

5. Bake uncovered in a 400° F. oven for about 15 minutes. Turn fillets halfway through their baking time.

****

There was a young fellow named Fisher,
Who was fishing for fish in a fissure,
A cod with a grin
Pulled the fisherman in,
Now they're fishing the fissure for Fisher.

Baked Carp

Carp fillets
2 1/2 cups canned tomatoes or tomato juice
1 onion, sliced
2 Tbsp. flour
1/2 tsp. salt
1/4 tsp. pepper
2 Tbsp. butter

1. Combine 2 1/2 cups canned tomatoes or tomato juice, 1/2 tsp. salt, 1/4 tsp. pepper and sliced onion.

2. Cook for 10 minutes then run through a sieve.

3. Melt 2 Tbsp. butter and add 2 Tbsp. flour.

5. Gradually add strained tomato mixture and stir until thickened.

6. Place carp fillets in a baking dish.

7. Pour mixture over carp steaks and bake at 350° F.

****

Hoosier Fried Carp

Carp fillets with mud vein removed
1/4 cup lemon juice
4 cups water
Corn meal
Flour
Salt

1. Score fillets 1/2-inch apart.

2. Soak a few hours or overnight in lemon juice
   and water.

3. Drain off solution, salt fish.

4. Coat fish in mixture of 1/2 corn meal and
   1/2 flour.

5. Fry in hot oil until flesh flakes with a fork.

****

You surely won't believe me,
I was fishing yesterday.
And the fish I got was bigger
Than the fish that got away.

Broiled Channel Catfish

2 lbs. skinless catfish fillets
1/4 cup French dressing
3 Tbsp. soy sauce
3/4 tsp. ginger, ground

1. Place fillets in a single layer, skinned side down, on a bake and serve platter, 10" by 16."

2. Combine French dressing, soy sauce, ginger.

3. Pour sauce over fillets and let stand 10 minutes.

4. Broil for about 10 to 15 minutes or until fillets flake easily when tested with a fork. Baste once during broiling with sauce in pan.

Fried Catfish Fillets

6 skinned, filleted catfish
2 tsp. salt
1/4 tsp. pepper
2 eggs
2 Tbsp. milk
2 cups cornmeal

1. Sprinkle both sides of the fillets with salt and pepper.

2. Beat eggs slightly and blend in milk.

3. Dip fish in the egg mixture and roll in cornmeal.

4. Place fish in a heavy frying pan which contains 1/8-inch of melted fat, hot but not smoking.

5. Fry at moderate heat. When fish is brown on one side, turn carefully and brown the other side.

Deep Fat Fried Fish and Potato Balls

This recipe is from the deep south and probably was developed to make less desirable fish more palatable, but you may use any freshwater variety. However, if there are certain fish you like less than others, give them a try with this recipe.

1 lb. boneless fillets
5 large potatoes
2 eggs
1/2 cup milk
2 Tbsp. onion, finely chopped
Salt and pepper

1. Peel the potatoes and quarter them.

2. Place the potatoes and the fish in a kettle and cover with cold water.

3. Bring to a boil and cook until the potatoes are done (easily penetrated with a fork). Skim from time to time if necessary.

4. Drain and then mash the potatoes and fish together.

5. Add the eggs to the milk and mix thoroughly.

6. Add this mixture to the fish and potatoes and again mix thoroughly.

7. Season to taste.

8. Form into small balls - no more than 1-inch in diameter.

9. Meanwhile, pre-heat cooking oil to about 400° F.

10. Deep fry the balls until golden brown.

Courtesy Duane R. Lund, *101 Favorite Fresh Fish Recipes*.

****

Beer Batter Catfish

Catfish fillets
1 cup flour or pancake mix
1 tsp. paprika
1 can beer (12 oz.)
Salt
Pepper
Garlic powder (to taste)

1. Mix beer and pancake mix.

2. Coat fish with flour, salt, pepper, garlic and
    paprika.

3. Dip fish into batter.

4. Fry in oil until brown on both sides. Drain on
    paper towels.

Easy Broiled Catfish

Skinned catfish fillets
1 packet dry onion soup
1/4 lb. butter
Juice of 1 lemon

1. Melt 1/4 lb. butter, add one packet dry onion soup mix and juice of one lemon.

2. Coat skinned catfish with mixture and wrap each one in aluminum foil.

3. Broil about 2 1/2 minutes each side over hot coals.

Baked Catfish Delight

4 catfish fillets
3 Tbsp. Dijon mustard
2 Tbsp. milk
1 cup pecans, ground

1. Combine mustard and milk in small bowl.

2. Dip fillets in mustard mixture, then dip in ground pecans, coating thoroughly. Shake off excess nuts.

3. Place fish on greased baking sheet.

4. Bake at 500° F. 10 to 12 minutes or until fish flakes easily with a fork.

Broiled Catfish Fillets

4 catfish fillets
1/2 tsp. garlic salt
1/2 tsp. lemon pepper
Lemon wedges

1. Sprinkle fillets with garlic salt and lemon pepper.

2. Preheat broiler pan 5 minutes then spray with nonstick coating.

3. Place fish on broiler pan. Broil about 4 to 6 minutes or until fish flakes easily.

4. Serve with lemon wedges.

****

If all the fish caught were as big as the stories told about them, sardines would have to be packed and sold in large garbage cans!

Southern Baked Catfish

2 lbs. catfish fillets, skinned
1 tsp. salt
Pepper to taste
1/2 cup green onion, diced
1 lemon, thinly sliced
1 Tbsp. parsley
1/2 cup ketchup
2 Tbsp. butter, melted
2 Tbsp. dry vermouth

1. Place the fillets in a shallow, greased baking dish.

2. Season with salt and pepper. Sprinkle the onions and parsley and layer the lemon slices over the fish.

3. Combine the remaining ingredients and pour over the fish.

4. Bake for 25 minutes in 350° F. oven.

****

A fisherman is a jerk at one end of the line waiting for a jerk at the other.

Angry wife

Mary's Barbecued Catfish

12 catfish fillets
1/8 tsp. paprika
1/2 cup salad oil
1/4 cup white vinegar
1/4 cup ketchup
2 Tbsp. sugar
1/4 tsp. salt
1/4 tsp. pepper
Melted butter

1. Brush fillets with melted butter.

2. Place on grill 3-to 4-inches from coals.

3. Combine other ingredients and mix well.

4. Coat fillets and cook for 5 minutes on each side or until done. Brush often with sauce.

Courtesy Mary Bronson, Lexington, Kentucky.

****

The carp is the queen of rivers: a stately, a good and very subtle fish.

Izaak Walton

Blackened Catfish

4 catfish fillets (preferably of equal thickness)
1/2 tsp. onion powder
1/2 tsp. garlic salt
1/2 tsp. red pepper, grounded
1/2 tsp. dried basil, crushed
1/4 tsp. white pepper, grounded
1/4 tsp. dried thyme, crushed
1/4 tsp. pepper
1/8 tsp. sage, grounded
1/4 cup butter, melted

1. In a small mixing bowl combine seasoning ingredients except butter.

2. Brush both sides of fish with some of the melted butter.

3. Coat both sides with seasonings.

4. Preheat the skillet 5 minutes or until a drop of water sizzles.

5. Place the coated fillets in skillet.

6. Drizzle about 2 tsp. of the melted butter over the fish.

7. Grill the fillets for about 2 1/2 to 3 minutes or until blackened.

8. Turn fish and drizzle with 2 tsp. of the melted butter. Grill another 2 1/2 minutes until blackened and fish flakes easily when tested with a fork.

Fish Cakes

1 cup shredded, leftover cooked fish,
   or 2 small cans tuna or salmon
1 tsp. prepared seafood seasoning
2 eggs, beaten
2 Tbsp. butter, melted
1 cup instant mashed potatoes, prepared
Fine, dry bread crumbs
Pepper to taste
Package dry instant onion soup mix

1. Shred the fish, removing all bones.

2. Mix butter into prepared mashed potatoes and add the fish, soup mix, and seasoning. Blend.

3. Add beaten eggs and mix well.

4. Form into patties. Dust with bread crumbs.

5. Fry in hot fat, turning once, until both sides are crisply browned. Serve with a sharp tomato sauce.

Fish Croquettes

2 cups flaked, cooked fish, poached or steamed
1/2 cup chopped mushrooms sautéed in 1 Tbsp. butter
1 small onion, minced
1 tsp. lemon juice
1 tsp. steak sauce
1/4 cup parsley, minced
1/4 cup celery, minced
1/2 tsp. chervil
1/2 tsp. dill weed
1/2 can cream of celery soup
1 egg, beaten
1 cup dried bread crumbs, rolled finely
2 Tbsp. butter

1. Blend together all ingredients except the egg, butter and dried bread crumbs.

2. Press the mixture into a pie pan and chill thoroughly.

3. Divide into 12 parts and shape into cone-shaped croquettes.

4. Dip in beaten egg and roll in bread crumbs.

5. Brown on all sides in butter and serve with a cheese mushroom sauce.

Fish Patties

Chop two cups of flaked boneless fish. Use most any fish which has already been cooked (trout, walleyes, northern, bass, etc.). This is a very good way of using left-overs. Combine the chopped fish with:

2 eggs
1/4 cup onion, chopped
1/4 cup water
Pinch of salt

1. Add cracker crumbs or bread crumbs until mixture has a consistency which can be easily molded into patties.

2. Fry on well-greased griddle or in a heavy frying pan until well-browned on both sides.

Courtesy Duane R. Lund, 101 Favorite Freshwater Fish Recipes.

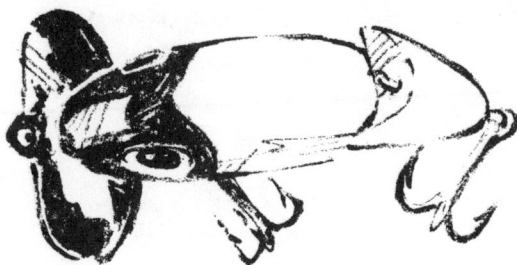

Savory Fish Cakes

4 cups raw fish, ground
1 tsp. mace
1 tsp. ginger
1 tsp. nutmeg
4 eggs
4 Tbsp. potato flour
4 cups milk
1 tsp. onion powder
1/2 tsp. garlic powder
Pepper
4 Tbsp. butter, melted
4 tsp. salt

1. Grind fish at least 3 times.

2. Put ground fish in large mixer bowl.

3. Mix slowly, add spices (not salt).

4. Add 1 egg at a time, beat thoroughly.

5. Mix potato flour in ice-cold milk and add to fish mixture slowly.

6. Add onion and garlic powder and pepper.

7. After mixture is thoroughly whipped, add melted butter and salt.

8. Brown fish cakes in half-butter and half-Crisco in 375° F. frying pan.

Lemon Stuffed Fish

4 fish fillets (1 1/2 lbs. each)
1/2 cup celery, finely chopped
1/4 cup onion, chopped
3 Tbsp. butter
4 cups dry bread cubes or croutons
1/2 tsp. lemon peel, grated
4 tsp. lemon juice
1 Tbsp. parsley, snipped
1 Tbsp. butter, melted

1. Place 2 fillets in a greased baking pan.

2. Cook celery and onion in 3 Tbsp. butter until crisp tender.

3. Pour over bread.

4. Add lemon peel and juice, parsley, 1/2 tsp. salt and a dash of pepper, then toss together.

5. Spoon half the stuffing mixture on each fillet in the pan.

6. Top with remaining two pieces of fish, brush with 1 Tbsp. butter. Sprinkle with salt and paprika and bake, covered at 350° F. for about 25 minutes.

Snapper Stew

1 3-lb snapping turtle, cut in pieces
1 jar Herb-ox chicken flavored bouillon crystals
Juice from 1 20-oz. can pineapple
3 carrots, cut into 1/2-inch pieces
4 potatoes, cut into 1/2-inch pieces
2 onions, cut into 1/2-inch pieces
1 cup frozen peas
2 bay leaves
1/4 cup flour
1/2 cup cold water

1. Bring turtle to boil in water. When it foams, rinse meat, pan and lid.

2. Use fresh hot water, add turtle, bullion crystals and juice of pineapple. Boil first on high, then to medium-high and cook until meat pulls from bone.

3. Remove meat, rinse in cold water, debone and place back in pot.

4. Add potatoes, peas, carrots, onions and bay leaves. Cook until vegetables are done.

5. Remove bay leaves. Mix water and flour and add to stew to thicken. Stew can be served over biscuits or noodles.

Courtesy Barb Kuder, Vicksburg, Michigan.

Poached Crappie Fillets

4 crappie fillets, (about 1 to 1 1/2 lbs.)
1/2 cup tomato juice
3 Tbsp. butter, cut into 1/4-inch pieces
2 Tbsp. green onion, finely chopped
1/4 tsp. salt
1/4 tsp. pepper

1. Fold fillets in half and arrange in a 10-inch round baking dish with the thicker portions facing outward.

2. Pour the tomato juice over the fish.

3. Dot the fillets with butter and sprinkle with the chopped onion, salt and pepper.

4. Cover with clear plastic wrap.

5. Microwave on high power for 5 to 7 1/2 minutes or until fish flakes easily with a fork. Let the dish stand covered for 4 minutes then check for doneness.

****

Nothing grows faster than a fish between the time it takes the bait and the time it gets away.

Crappie Casserole

2 lbs. crappie fillets
1/2 lb. mild cheddar cheese
Small bag potato chips
1 bottle ranch dressing

1. Coat fillets with salad dressing, and place in casserole dish.

2. Sprinkle grated cheese over the fillets.

3. Crush potato chips and sprinkle over fish.

4. Bake in preheated, 350° F. oven for 15 minutes.

Zesty Broiled Crappie

6 large crappie fillets
1/2 lb. butter, melted
Juice of 6 limes
Salt and pepper
12 raw shrimp (peeled, deveined and minced)
Black pepper, milled

1. Mix 3/4 cup butter, juice of 4 limes, shrimp and pepper. Blend well.

2. Place fillets on broiler, spoon sauce over fish and broil for 12 minutes, basting with sauce often.

3. Sprinkle hot lime juice over hot plates, place fish on plates, brush with hot melted butter and sprinkle with salt and pepper to taste.

Fried Crappie Delight

2 lbs. crappie fillets
3 eggs, beaten
1 tsp. ginger, grated
3 Tbsp. butter
2 Tbsp. soy sauce
2 Tbsp. green onion, chopped
3 Tbsp. dry or medium sherry
3 Tbsp. cornstarch

1. Mix the eggs, cornstarch, ginger, soy sauce, onion and sherry thoroughly.

2. Dip the fillets in batter and fry quickly in hot butter.

****

He angled many a purling brook
But lacked an angler's skill:
He lied about the fish he took,
And here he's lying still.

Tombstone Inscription

Barbecued Crappie

1 lb. crappie fillets
2 Tbsp. soy sauce
1 Tbsp. lemon juice
1/2 cup sour cream
1/2 cup sesame seeds, toasted
3/4 cup corn flakes crumbs
Salt and pepper

1. Brush fillets with mixture of soy sauce and lemon juice.

2. Season with salt and pepper.

3. Coat both sides with sour cream.

4. Combine sesame seeds and corn flakes. Roll the fillets in crumb mixture.

5. Place fillets on broiler pan and broil for 5 to 10 minutes. Turn once.

****

"I'm going out to fish," Simon Peter told them, and they said, "We'll go with you." John 21:3 (NIV)

Oven Baked Crappie

1 lb. crappie fillets
1/4 cup parmesan cheese
1/2 cup oleo
2/3 cup cornflakes
1/2 tsp. basil
1/2 tsp. salt
1/4 tsp. garlic powder
1/2 tsp. oregano

1. Mix all dry ingredients.

2. Dip fillets in melted oleo, then in crumb mixture.

2. Bake at 350° F. for 25 to 30 minutes.

Crispy Crappie

2 lbs. crappie fillets
2 tsp. garlic salt
1 1/2 tsp. onion powder
48 round buttery crackers, finely crushed (2 cups)
1/2 cup beer
1 egg, beaten
Vegetable oil

1. Combine garlic salt and onion powder.

2. Sprinkle fillets with 1/2 teaspoon garlic-onion mixture.

3. Mix remainder with cracker crumbs on a sheet of aluminum foil.

4. Combine beer and egg in shallow dish.

5. Place fillets in beer mixture.

6. Coat both sides with seasoned cracker crumbs.

7. In fry pan, heat 1/8-to 1/4-inch vegetable oil over medium-high heat.

8. Fry fillets 3 to 5 minutes on first side then turn.

9. Fry second side until golden brown and fish flakes with a fork.

****

A fish out of water must feel like a moth in a nudist colony.

Fish Chowder

6 slices bacon
3 large potatoes
2 cans minced clams or 1 lb. of de-boned fish (fresh
    or saltwater)
2 medium onions
1 quart milk
Salt, pepper and butter to taste

1. Fry bacon crisp. Crumble.

2. Dice potatoes and onions.

3. Sauté the onions in the bacon fat until transparent.

4. Put fish in soup pot with potatoes, onions and ba-
    con. Season lightly.

5. Add enough water to cover and simmer until fish
    and potatoes are done.

6. Add milk and simmer for 15 minutes. Do not boil.

7. Add further seasoning if needed. Can vary taste by
    adding a small amount of sugar. Serve hot.

Courtesy Jack Cooper, Indianapolis, Indiana.

Fried Fish Fillets

4 - 6 fish fillets
1/4 cup flour
1 tsp. salt
1 egg
2 Tbsp. water
1/2 cup fine bread or cracker crumbs

1. Mix water with egg and beat.

2. Mix salt and four.

3. Dip fillets in salted flour, then the egg mix and then in fine crumbs.

4. Fry fish until it flakes easily.

Courtesy of Vera Truman, Warsaw, Indiana.

Fish Hash

2 cups cold fish, flaked
2 cups cold boiled potatoes, diced
1 Tbsp. onion, minced
1 egg, beaten
1/2 tsp. salt
1/4 tsp. pepper

1. Combine all the ingredients and fry in salt pork fat until golden brown. Fold and serve like an omelet.

Indiana Fish Chowder

1 to 1 1/2 lbs. fish
2 Tbsp. bacon fat
1 large onion, chopped
1/2 cup celery, diced or 1 tsp. celery seeds
3 cups water
4 medium-size potatoes, peeled and sliced
1/4 tsp. seasoning salt
Dash pepper
1/4 tsp. dried thyme
2 tsp. dehydrated parsley flakes

1. Cut the fish into 1-inch pieces.

2. Heat the bacon fat in a large ironware skillet or Dutch oven and add the onion and celery.

3. Cook the chopped vegetables until the onion is limp and golden.

4. Add the water, then the sliced potatoes.

5. Add the salt, pepper, thyme and parsley, and stir.

6. Add the fish pieces and cover the pot. Cook for 20 minutes, until the fish flakes easily.

Crappie Spectacular

3 lb. large crappie fillets
5 Tbsp. olive or vegetable oil
1 1/2 cups onions, chopped
1/2 cup parsley, chopped
2 cups canned tomatoes
1 tsp. salt
2 cloves garlic, minced
1/4 tsp. pepper
1/2 cup white wine (optional)
Salt
Pepper

1. Season fish with salt and pepper. Let stand.

2. Sauté onions in oil until soft.

3. Add garlic, tomatoes, parsley, salt and pepper.

4. Cook 10 minutes.

5. Pour half of tomato sauce in baking dish 9" by 13."

6. Place fish on top, and cover with remaining sauce.

7. Pour wine over fish.

8. Bake in oven at 350° F. for 40 minutes (or until fish flakes with a fork). Baste often.

Beer Batter Crappies

4 lbs. crappie fillets
2 eggs, slightly beaten
1 cup flour
2/3 cup beer
2 Tbsp. oil
1/2 tsp. Tabasco
1/2 tsp. salt

1. Combine all ingredients and mix well.

2. Dip fish fillets into batter then drain.

3. Fry 2 to 3 minutes in hot oil.

Poor Man's Lobster

1. Cut northern pike fillets into bit-sized chunks.

2. Boil 2 quarts of water seasoned with 2 Tbsp. salt.

3. Drop fish chunks into the boiling water and cook until the fish flakes easily with a fork.

4. Remove, sprinkle with melted butter and lemon juice. Salt to taste.

Northern Pike Snacks

Northern pike fillets
1/2 lemon
2 slices onion
Salt
Pepper
2-3 bay leaves
Caraway seed

1. Fill sauce pan half full of water.

2. Cut pike into medium sized pieces and boil until flesh is white.

3. Rinse and chill overnight.

4. Serve cold with shrimp sauce.

****

The doc told the fisherman that he had only six months to live.
"Well," the angler said, "I guess I'll give up fishing and become a socialist."
"Why" asked the doctor.
"Because," the doomed angler replied. "It's better one of them should die than one of us."

Baked Northern Pike

4 lbs. pike fillets
1/2 cup butter, melted
1 cup cream
1 cup white wine
Juice of 1 lemon
1 large onion, sliced
Salt

1. Salt fish, cover with onion slices and let stand 1 hour.

2. Place in roasting pan and cover with melted butter, cream, wine and lemon juice.

3. Bake at 350° F. for 30 to 45 minutes. Baste frequently.

Fish Stock

Prepare fish stock for use in other recipes. This is a Finnish recipe.

2 to 3 lbs. fish trimmings, bones, head meat (or the whole head),
2 large onions, sliced
3 stalks celery
3 bay leaves
12 peppercorns
1 Tbsp. minced dill and/or other spices such as tarragon or thyme
White wine (optional)

1. Clean all fish parts. If you use heads, crack them with a hammer. If you choose not to use them, cut out the cheeks and use them.

2. Place all ingredients in a cooking pot.

3. Cover with water (If you use wine, cover with equal parts of water and wine).

4. Bring to a boil and then reduce heat; let simmer for about 1 1/2 hours.

5. Skim off any foam or solids that come to the surface.

6. Strain through a very fine mesh screen or cloth.

7. Keep the liquids and discard the solids. The liquid may be frozen for future use.

Courtesy Duane R. Lund, <u>Sauces, Seasonings and Marinades for Fish and Wild Game</u>.

Poor Man's Shrimp

1/2 lb. bite-sized strips or chunks of perch or walleye. (Bass or pike can be used as well)

1. Boil in saucepan with sufficient water, steam in pressure cooker or bake in microwave until just done.

2. Do not overcook and do not season.

3. Remove and chill for several hours.

4. Serve with favorite cocktail sauce as you would shrimp.

Courtesy Jack Cooper, Indianapolis, Indiana.

****

It is quite true that some men, when they tell a fish story, will go to any length.

Baked Perch Parmesan

Perch fillets
Bacon strips
Parsley, chopped
Olive oil
Salt and pepper
Cracker crumbs
Fresh parmesan cheese, grated
Lemon juice or white wine

1. Rub the fillets with olive oil or butter, salt and pepper.

2. Place the fish on strips of bacon in a baking dish, add some lemon juice or a little white wine to the top.

3. Mix parsely with cracker crumbs and parmesan cheese.

4. Bake until the fish flakes easily. When done, pour the sauce over the top, then add a little more cheese if desired.

****

My uncle watched a man fall out of a boat and go down twice under the water. When the man came for the third time, he said, "When you go down the next time, see if my bait is still on the hook."

Perch Tempura

2 lbs. fresh perch fillets
1 lemon, halved
1/2 Tempura batter* recipe
1 qt. vegetable oil

1. Cut fish fillets into bite-sized pieces and drain well on paper toweling.

2. Season with salt and squeeze lemon juice over the fish.

3. Spear pieces of fish and dip in the batter, drain slightly.

4. Fry in oil heated to 360° F. for about 5 minutes, turning to brown evenly.

*Tempura batter

2 cups sifted flour
3 egg yolks
2 cups ice water

1. Sift the flour 3 times.

2. Combine the egg yolks and water in a large bowl over ice and beat with a whisk until well blended.

3. Add the flour gradually, stirring and turning the mixture from the bottom with a spoon.

4. Do not over mix. The flour should be visible on top of the batter. Keep the batter over ice while dipping and frying.

Courtesy Duane R. Lund, <u>101 Favorite Freshwater Fish Recipes</u>.

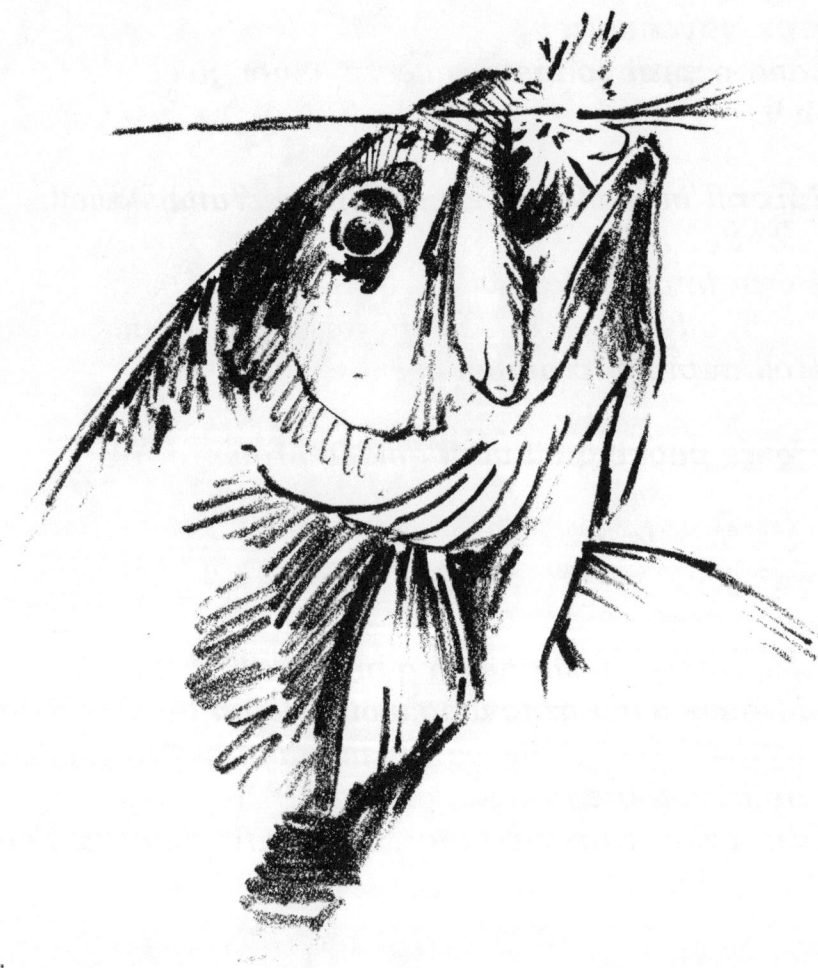

Perch And Pineapple

Here's a Hawaiian treatment for midwest fish.

1 lb. perch fillets (or other freshwater fish)
1/2 cup pineapple juice
1 Tbsp. lime juice
2 tsp. Worcestershire sauce
1/2 tsp. salt

1.   Cut fish into serving size portions. Place in a shallow baking dish.

2.   Combine pineapple juice, lime juice, Worcestershire sauce, salt and a dash of pepper. Pour over fish marinate for 1 hour, turning once.

3.   Drain, reserving marinade.

4.   Place fillets on a greased rack of a broiler pan.

5.   Broil 4-inches from heat until fish flakes. Brush occasionally with marinade.

6.   Heat remaining marinade and spoon over fish before serving.

Courtesy Duane R. Lund, <u>101 Favorite Freshwater Recipes</u>.

Baked Winona Lake Perch

1 lb. perch fillets
3/4 cup corn flakes
1 Tbsp. sesame seeds
3/4 tsp. ground ginger
1 egg
1 Tbsp. teriyaki sauce
1/2 tsp. vegetable oil

1. Crush cereal to coarse consistency.

2. Add sesame seeds and ginger.

3. Beat egg and add teriyaki sauce.

4. Dip fillets in egg mixture, then in cereal mixture.

5   Place fillets on baking pan that has been lightly coated with vegetable oil.

6. Bake at 450° F. 10 minutes per inch of thickness of fillets.

****

Fisherman's wife to her husband. "You spend so much time on fishing, I want a mink."
"Sure," the angler said. "I'll get you one, but you've got to keep the cage clean!"

Pan Fried Perch

1 lb. perch fillets
2 Tbsp. butter or margarine
2 Tbsp. shortening
1/2 cup flour
10 soda crackers, finely crushed
2 eggs
2 Tbsp. milk
Salt
Pepper

1. Beat eggs with milk in a bowl.

2. In separate dish combine flour, soda crackers, salt and pepper to taste.

3. Dip perch in egg mixture and then in flour mixture.

4. Melt butter and shortening in frying pan.

5. Place fish in pan and cook until fillets flake easily when tested with a fork.

****

The first bait casting reels were marketed in 1835 and the telephone invented in 1875. If you lived in 1835 you could have fished for 40 years without having the phone to ring a single time!

Perch Almondine

1 lb. perch fillets
1 stick butter or margarine
4 oz. almonds, sliced
1/4 cup lemon juice

1. Bake perch fillets until done at 325° F.

2. Melt 1 stick of butter or margarine.

3. Add 4-oz. sliced almonds.

4. Cook in a small kettle on stove top slowly until you
    are able to smell the almonds.

5. Add 1/4 cup lemon juice.

6. Pour over fish and serve immediately.

****

A fisherman boasted that he'd caught a 20 lb. salmon
and his neighbor asked if there had been any witness-
es. "Of course," he replied, "otherwise it would have
weighed 40 lbs.

Michigan Fried Smelt

2 lbs. cleaned smelt
1 1/2 tsp. salt
Dash of pepper
1 cup pancake mix
1/4 cup yellow cornmeal
1/2 tsp. salt (for batter)
1 1/4 cups milk
1/2 cup flour

1. Sprinkle smelt inside and out with salt and pepper.

2. Combine pancake mix, corn meal, and 1/2 tsp. salt.

3. Add milk and stir until blended.

4. Roll smelt in flour and dip in batter.

5. Arrange smelt in a single layer in a frying basket and fry in oil at 350° F. for 3 to 4 minutes or until browned.

****

A young angler was about to go fishing with his grandpa, so they proceeded to dig for worms in grandpa's garden.

After a while the youngster began to tire.

"Grandpa," he queried wearily, "whatever made you bury these things anyway?"

Pan Fried Smelt

2 lbs. cleaned smelt
1/2 cup cornmeal
1/2 cup flour
1 Tbsp. salt
1/2 tsp. pepper

1. Dip smelt in water, then coat with a mixture of
    cornmeal, flour, salt and pepper.

2. Fry in hot oil about 4 to 5 minutes on each side,
    until browned.

Colorado Rainbow Trout

6 rainbow trout fillets
1/4 cup oil
1/4 cup sesame seeds
2 Tbsp. lemon juice
1/2 tsp. salt,
Dash pepper

1. Combine all ingredients except trout.

2. Place fillets on a well-greased broiler pan.

3. Baste fish with sauce.

4. Cook about 4-inches from moderately hot heat for 5 to 8 minutes.

5. Turn and cook for 5 to 8 minutes longer or until fish flakes easily with a fork.

Bacon-fried Trout

Rainbow or brown trout
Mustard powder
Salt and pepper
Flour
Bacon fat
Garlic
Lemon juice

1. Rub the trout with mustard powder and sprinkle the inside with salt and pepper.

2. Place flour, salt and pepper in a paper bag and put the fish inside and shake.

3. Melt the bacon fat with the crushed garlic.

4. Cook the fillets in the bacon fat until the fish flakes easily.

5. Squeeze lemon juice over the fish.

6. Garnish with bacon slices and mint leaves.

Trout Almondine

4 rainbow trout fillets
4 Tbsp. butter
Juice of 2 lemons
1/2 cup blanched almonds, sliced
Salt
Pepper, freshly ground
Parsley

1. Rub trout with butter and sprinkle with salt and
    freshly ground pepper.

2. Pour lemon juice over fish.

3. Place in a greased baking dish.

4. Bake in a 425° F. oven for about 10 minutes
    or until fish flakes easily.

5. While the trout is baking, melt the rest of
    the butter in a saucepan and add the almonds
    and cook until they are brown.

6. Pour the butter and browned almonds over the
    fillets before serving.

****

Walleye with Cashew Nuts

6 walleye fillets
1/2 cup cashew nuts, chopped
2 tsp. lemon rind, grated
2 Tbsp. lemon juice
Butter
Flour
Parsley
Salt and pepper

1. Put the juice and rind of lemon in a dish and marinate the fish for 20 minutes.

2. Roll the fish in seasoned flour and fry in oil or butter until fish flakes easily.

3. Remove the fish, set aside and in the same pan fry the cashew nuts until lightly browned.

4. Sprinkle the fish with lemon juice and the browned nuts.

****

127

Sweet-and-Sour Walleye

1 lb. walleye fillets
1/2 cup lemon juice
1/2 tsp. salt
1/4 cup salad oil
1/2 tsp. pepper
2 Tbsp. onion, grated
1 tsp. dry mustard
2 Tbsp. brown sugar

1. Mix all ingredients (except fillets), stirring until sugar is completely dissolved.

2. Place fish in heat-proof broiler platter and pour sauce over the top.

3. Preheat oven broiler and place fillets about 4-inches from heat.

4. Broil about 3 minutes, turn and broil about 5 minutes or until fish flakes easily with a fork. Baste frequently during cooking time.

****

What fish makes sweet sandwiches?
"Jellyfish!"

Broiled Walleye Fillets

2 lbs. walleye fillets
2 cups cornflakes
1/2 tsp. lemon pepper
1/2 tsp. oregano
1/4 tsp. garlic powder

1. Crush the cornflakes into crumbs.

2. Mix all the dry ingredients.

3. Dip fillets in vegetable oil and roll in the crumb
    mixture.

4. Place fillets on greased broiling pan and broil until
    fish flakes.

Simmered Walleye

6 walleye fillets
2 cups water
1/2 cup vinegar
3 onions, sliced thin
2 lemons, sliced with peel on
1/2 stick butter
6 cloves garlic

1. Place all ingredients except the fillets in a deep cooking dish.

2. Position the fillets on top of ingredients.

3. Cover and simmer 12 to 20 minutes.

4. Salt and pepper to taste.

Walleye Au Gratin

4 walleye fillets
2 Tbsp. cracker crumbs
1 can tomatoes
2 Tbsp. onion, grated
1/4 tsp. salt
1/4 tsp. pepper
1 Tbsp. butter
1/2 cup cheddar cheese, grated

1. Roll fish fillets in cracker crumbs, place in greased baking pan.

2. Combine tomatoes, onion and seasonings and pour over the fish and dot with butter.

3. Bake 35 minutes or until fish flakes.

4. Sprinkle with cheddar cheese.

Spicy Walleye Snacks

2 walleye fillets cut into bit-sized pieces
1 cup boiling water
1 Tbsp. sugar
1 tsp. 5-spice powder
Lettuce leaves

1. Combine the boiling water, sugar and 5-spice powder in a small bowl.

2. Deep fry fish in hot peanut oil until brown, but not burned.

3. Dip each piece for 20 seconds in the mixture.

4. Serve pieces on lettuce on a warm platter.

5. Dip in a sweet-and-sour sauce.

Orange Walleye Delight

1 lb. walleye fillets
1/4 cup white wine
1/4 cup orange juice
4 tsp. butter
Grated rind of 1 orange
1 tsp. salt
1/4 tsp. pepper
1 orange, peeled and sliced

1. Place fillets in an oiled casserole dish.

2. Mix together the white wine and orange juice and pour over the fish.

3. Allow to marinate for 1/2 hour.

4. Blend the grated rind with the butter and dot on the fish.

5. Sprinkle on the salt and pepper.

6. Cover the dish and bake in a 350° F. oven for about 1/2 hour.

7. Serve garnished with orange slices.

****

Deep Fried Walleye

2 lb. walleye fillets
Ritz Crackers
4 eggs
1 cup flour
2 Tbsp. lemon juice
2 Tbsp. milk

1.   Roll Ritz Crackers to make crumbs.

2.   Mix egg, lemon juice and milk.

3.   Dust fillets with flour.

4.   Dip the fish into the egg mixture.

5.   Coat the fillets with cracker crumbs.

6.   Deep fry at 325° F. until golden brown or fish flakes.

Courtesy Gloria Bradway, Warsaw, Indiana.

****

My friend, Achish Featherbelt, gave up on ice fishing last year. By the time he cut a hole in the ice big enough to put his boat in, he was too tired to fish.

Pickled Fish - A

Fillet fish and cut into 1 1/2-inch pieces. Bring 4 cups of water to boil and 1 tsp. salt. Drop about 6 pieces of fish into boiling water at a time. Boil 1 minute. Drain. Then in pyrex bowl alternate layers of fish and sliced onion. Add to this 1/2 tsp. whole pickling spice. Bring to a boil: 4 cups white vinegar, 2 cups water, 1 cup sugar, 1/2 cup plus 1 Tbsp. salt. Pour this over fish, let stand till cooled. Keep refrigerated.

Pickled Fish - B

Place left-over fish in bowl. In a skillet add 2 Tbsp. oil, medium sliced onion, 4 or 5 leaves of sage and simmer for a few minutes until onion is tender. In a sauce pan, heat 1 cup wine vinegar, and 1 cup water. When hot, pour into skillet and stir and then pour over fish. The liquid should almost cover fish. Cool and place in refrigerator.

Pickled Fish - C

To each quart of fish add 5/8 cup of salt. Cover with white vinegar and let stand 5 days. Wash fish twice and pack in jar with one layer fish and one layer of onions alternately. Place 1 Tbsp. mixed pickling spice and cover with 2 parts white vinegar and 1 part of sugar warmed. Allow at least 3 days for curing.

SEAFOOD

Jersey Bluefish Cakes

2-1/2 cups cooked blue fish, flaked
1 cup potatoes, mashed
1/2 tsp. parsley flakes
1/4 tsp. dry mustard
1/4 tsp. salt
1 egg
1/4 tsp. onion powder
Flour as needed
Dash cayenne pepper

1.   *Mix all ingredients, except egg and flour, until blended.*

2.   *Add egg and mix well.*

3.   *Shape into 6 or 8 patties, roll in flour.*

4.   *Refrigerate 30 to 60 minutes.*

5.   *Pan fry in oil until golden. Turn over and repeat.*

****

Mustard Broiled Bluefish

2 bluefish fillets (1 lb. each)
1/4 cup Dijon mustard
1/4 cup lime juice
3 Tbsp. water
3 Tbsp. fresh parsley, chopped
1/2 tsp. hot pepper sauce
1/4 tsp. garlic powder
2 large onions, sliced

1. Place fillets in shallow glass dish.

2. Combine mustard, lime juice, water, parsley, hot pepper sauce and garlic powder; pour over fish.

3. Cover and refrigerate 45 minutes.

4. Place onion slices in greased broiler pan.

5. Remove fish from marinade; place fillets on top of onion slices and then place more onion slices on top of the fillets.

6. Broil for 15 to 20 minutes or until fish flakes easily with fork.

****

Clam Patties

1 1/4 cups clams, minced
2 cups potatoes, cooked and mashed
2 Tbsp. butter or margarine
1/2 tsp. salt
1/4 tsp. pepper
1 Tbsp. lemon juice
2 eggs, slightly beaten

1. Drain minced clams and combine with mashed potatoes, butter, salt, pepper and lemon juice.

2. Add beaten eggs, mix well.

3. Shape into 12 patties of equal size and fry in hot oil until lightly browned on both sides.

New England Clam Chowder

1 pint clams
1 cup clam liquid and water
1/4 cup bacon or salt pork, chopped
1/4 cup onion, chopped
1 cup potatoes, diced
2 cups milk
1/2 tsp. salt
Dash pepper
Parsley

1. Drain clams and save liquid.

2. Chop clams.

3. Fry bacon until slightly brown, add onion
    and cook until tender.

4. Add clam liquid, potatoes, seasonings and clams.

5. Cook about 15 minutes or until potatoes
    are tender.

6. Add milk and heat.

7. Garnish with chopped parsley sprinkled on top.

8. If needed, it can be thickened slightly with
    cornstarch mixed with water.

Manhattan Clam Chowder - A

1 pint clams and liquid
1 small onion, chopped
1/4 cup green pepper, chopped
1/2 cup celery, diced
3 cups water
1/2 cup carrots, diced
3 cups potatoes, diced
1 tsp. salt
3 cups canned tomatoes
1/8 tsp. thyme
2 Tbsp. parsley, chopped

1. Sauté onion, pepper and celery.

2. Add water, carrots and potatoes, salt,
     tomatoes and thyme.

3. Simmer 20 minutes.

4. Add clams and simmer 5 minutes longer.

5. Sprinkle with parsley.

****

Since our earth is 2/3 water and only 1/3 land, it seems
only logical that we should spend 2/3 of our time
fishing and 1/3 working.

Manhattan Clam Chowder - B

2 cups clams, minced
1/2 lb. salt pork, diced
3 cups water
1 can tomatoes
1 large onion, diced
1 green pepper, diced
1 cup raw potatoes, diced
2 tsp. salt
1 cup raw carrots, diced
1 cup celery, diced
1/4 tsp pepper
1/2 cup fine cracker crumbs

1. Cook pork in a Dutch oven until lightly brown.

2. Add onion and cook until golden brown.

3. Add remaining vegetables, water and
    seasonings.

4. Cover and simmer 1 hour.

5. Add clams and cook 5 minutes.

6. Add cracker crumbs.

Jersey Clam Fritters

1 pint clams
2 eggs
1/3 cup milk
1 1/3 cups flour
2 tsp. baking powder
Salt and pepper to taste

1. Chop clams finely and drain.

2. Beat eggs until light and frothy.

3. Add gradually milk alternated with flour which has been sifted with baking powder, salt and pepper.

4. Beat continuously.

5. Add clams and mix thoroughly.

6. Measure out Tbsp. amounts and place in hot oil (375° F.).

7. Drain on absorbent paper.

8. Serve with lemon wedges and tartar sauce.

Deviled Clams

12 clams
1 cup clam juice
2 medium size onions
1/2 loaf bread, crumbled
3 hard cooked eggs, chopped
1 Tbsp. parsley, minced
1 egg, beaten
Dash Worcestershire sauce
1 oz. butter, browned

1. Put clams through a food chopper with onions.

2. Add the bread bits, chopped eggs, and parsley; mix thoroughly.

3. Combine Worcestershire sauce, beaten egg and browned butter.

4. Combine mixtures and moisten with clam juice.

5. Fill buttered clam shells and bake until brown.

****

Clam Croquettes

1 cup clams, chopped
2 Tbsp. butter
4 Tbsp. flour
1/2 cup milk
1 egg, beaten
Salt and paprika
1 tsp. parsley, minced
1 tsp. onion, minced
1 egg, hard boiled and chopped
Bread crumbs

1. Cream butter and flour then gradually add milk and beaten egg.

2. Cook until thick. Season with salt and paprika.

3. Add onion, chopped clams and hard boiled egg.

4. When mixture is cool, form into cone shapes and roll in bread crumbs, beaten egg and again in bread crumbs.

5. Fry in hot fat until golden brown.

6. Drain and serve with lemon wedges and sprigs of crisp water cress.

Clam Bisque

15 or 20 clams, chopped

1. Simmer in juice for 15 minutes and skim.

2. Make a white sauce of:

    a. 2 Tbsp. butter
    b. 2 Tbsp. flour
    c. 2 cups milk
    d. 1 tsp. onion, grated
    e. 1/2 tsp. celery salt
    f. 1/4 tsp. paprika

3. Just before serving time, combine mixtures and re-heat to boiling point. Do not boil.

****

The fisherman sliced off a hunk of baloney for a sandwich during a lull in fishing. A fly landed on the greasy knife handle, filled up with baloney grease and then dropped dead. His buddy watched the episode and said, "Hey, Mac, d'ja see that?"

"Sure," Mac said. "it shows, never fly off the handle when you're full of baloney."

Atlantic City Baked Cod

2 cups cod, flaked
2 Tbsp. butter
2 Tbsp. flour
1 1/4 cups tomato juice
1 Tbsp. onion, chopped
1 Tbsp. green pepper, chopped
1/2 cup bread crumbs

1. Melt the butter in a skillet, gradually stir in flour and add tomato juice, stirring constantly as it thickens.

2. Add onion and green pepper.

3. Remove from heat and stir in flaked fish.

4. Pour into a greased casserole.

5. Mix melted butter with bread crumbs and spread on top.

6. Bake for 15 minutes in a 400° F. oven or until bread crumbs are brown.

****

Bill Backlash ordered a tuna fish sandwich at Harvey's Heartburn Haven and got Charlie.

Curried Cod Delight

2 lbs. cod fillets
1 cup celery, finely sliced
1/2 cup onion, sliced
1 Tbsp. melted fat or oil
3/4 cup milk
1/2 tsp. curry powder
1 tsp. salt
Dash of pepper
Paprika

1. Place fillets in a single layer on the bottom of a greased baking dish.

2. Cook celery and onion in fat for 5 minutes in a saucepan.

3. Mix celery and onion with seasonings and milk. Spread over fish.

4. Bake at 350° F. for 25 to 30 minutes.

5. Sprinkle with paprika and garnish with parsley.

****

I taught my pet fish to sing, but lately he's been singing off key...and you know how hard it is to "tuna fish!"

Crab Cakes

1 lb. crab meat
1 egg
Dash Tabasco
1 tsp. mustard
Celery, chopped
Onions, minced
Bread crumbs
1 Tbsp. mayonnaise
Salt and pepper to taste

1. Mix all ingredients (except bread crumbs) well.

2. Form into patties.

3. Roll in bread crumbs.

4. Fry in cooking oil until golden brown.

****

Two fishermen sitting on a bridge, their lines in the water, made a bet as to who would catch the first fish. One of them got a bite on his line and got so excited that he fell off the bridge.

"Oh, well," said the other, "if you're going to dive for them, the bet's off."

Boston Deviled Crab

1 lb. crab meat
1 large onion, chopped fine
6 sprigs celery, chopped fine
4 Tbsp. butter
1 tsp. hot sauce
1/2 tsp. oregano
1/4 tsp. dried mustard
1 Tbsp. Worcestershire sauce
1 Tbsp. pimento, chopped
1 cup water
Salt and pepper to taste
12 soda crackers, finely crushed

1. Sauté onions and celery in butter.

2. Stir in seasonings and crab meat; mix well over low flame.

3. Add cracker crumbs and water, blending thoroughly.

4. Place in baking casserole, top with buttered bread crumbs, and bake at 350° F. for 30 minutes or until crumbs are brown.

****

Jersey Crab Burgers

1 lb. crab meat
1 egg
1/2 cup onion, chopped
1 stalk celery, chopped
1 Tbsp. parsley, chopped
Salt and pepper to taste
Bisquick

1. Put crab meat into a bowl.

2. Add unbeaten egg, onion, celery, parsley, and seasonings. Blend carefully.

3. Add just enough Bisquick to coat mixture.

4. Drop full tablespoons into hot fat.

5. Serve in hamburger rolls.

****

Willie Woodchip, whose mental elevator usually stops one floor short of the top, went fishing in Canada for two weeks with his friend, Hiram Hackood. They caught only one fish.

When they got home, Hiram said, "The way I figure our expenses, that fish cost us $600."

"Well," said Willie, "at that price, it's a good thing we didn't catch any more."

Delicate Crab Soup

1 can condensed tomato soup
1 can condensed pea soup
1 can consommé
1 lb. crab meat
Salt and pepper
Sherry wine

1. Combine first three ingredients in a double boiler, add crab meat and heat over the hot water for 1/2 hour.

2. Before serving, season to taste and add sherry wine.

Hot Crab Meat Puffs

2 cups crab meat
2 egg whites
1 cup mayonnaise
1 Tbsp. Worcestershire sauce
Toast fingers (one side)

1. Beat egg whites until stiff, fold in mayonnaise, crab meat, and seasonings.

2. Place generous portions on toast fingers (untoasted side), sprinkle with paprika and broil until puffy and brown. Serve hot.

Baked Flounder

1 lb. baby flounder
Mayonnaise
1 1/2 cup Italian bread crumbs
1/2 cup parmesan cheese

1. Mix together bread crumbs and cheese.

2. Coat one side of fish with mayonnaise (thick).

3. Place in bread crumbs.

4. Coat other side with mayonnaise and place
    in bread crumbs. Make sure it is well-coated.

5. Place in buttered baking dish and bake at 350° F.
    until the fish flakes easily with a fork.

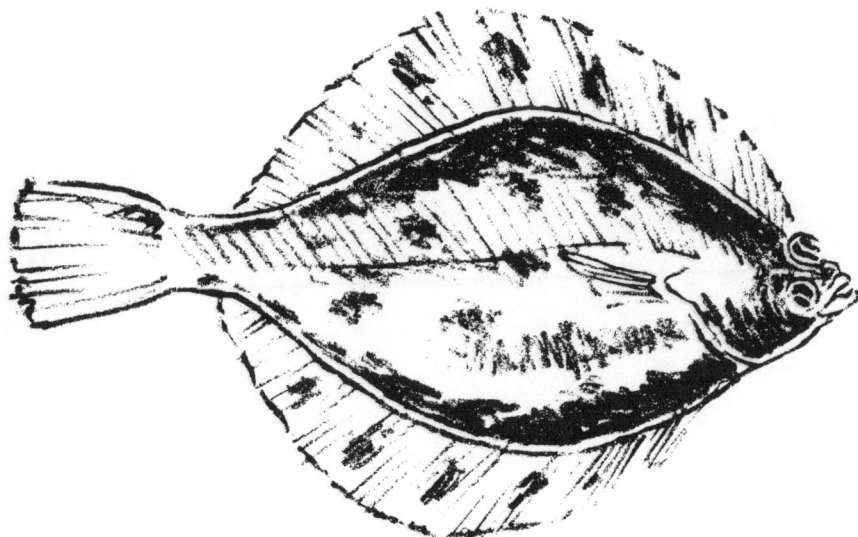

Flounder Parmesan

1 lb. flounder fillets
1/2 cup commercial sour cream
2 Tbsp. parmesan cheese, grated
2 Tbsp. minced onion
1 Tbsp. lemon juice
1/2 tsp. garlic powder
1/2 tsp. salt
1/4 tsp. pepper
Paprika
Fresh parsley sprigs

1. Place fillets in a lightly greased 9" by 13" baking dish.

2. Combine remaining ingredients, paprika and parsley in a small mixing bowl, stirring well. Spread on fillets.

3. Bake at 375° F. for 20 minutes or until fish flakes easily with a fork.

4. Place fillets in a serving platter; sprinkle with paprika and garnish with parsley.

****

Fisherman: A gent who, by exaggeration, makes it a lot easier to swallow a fish bone than his latest fish story.

Pan Fried Flounder

1 lb. flounder fillets
1/2 cup flour
1/2 cup corn starch
2 tsp. baking powder
1 Tbsp. sugar
1/4 tsp. salt
1/2 cup ice water
1 egg, beaten

1. Mix flour, corn starch, baking powder, sugar, and salt together.

2. Combine water and egg in a bowl.

3. Carefully stir dry ingredients into egg mixture, leaving air bubbles.

4. Heat about 2-inches of oil in skillet.

5. Dip fillets into the batter and brown in oil on one side, turn and brown on other side.

6. Drain fillets on paper towels. Serve with tartar sauce.

****

Flounder and Lemon

4 small founder fillets
3 Tbsp. butter
2 small onions
2 lemons
Salt and pepper
Parsley

1. Season the fish lightly and place the fillets on a piece of greased aluminum foil.

2. Slice the onions thinly and place over the fish together with sliced lemons.

3   Top with the remaining butter and wrap the foil around the fish firmly.

4. Place on a baking tray and bake in moderate oven for about 35 minutes.

5. When ready to serve, open foil and sprinkle with parsley.

****

"What fish is a member of a singing group?"
"Bass!"

Flounder With Dill Sauce

1/2 lbs. flounder fillets
1 can chicken broth
3 Tbsp. lemon juice
1 Tbsp. corn starch
3 Tbsp. dried dill weed

1.   In skillet, over medium-high heat, heat 1 1/4 cups chicken broth to a boil; reduce heat.

2.   Add fish; cover and simmer 2 to 3 minutes or until fish flakes easily with fork.

3.   Carefully remove fish with slotted spoon to heated serving platter.

4.   Meanwhile, in small saucepan, blend remaining broth and lemon juice into cornstarch.

5.   Cook over medium-high heat, stirring, until mixture thickens and boils.

6.   Boil 1 minute; stir in dill. To serve, spoon sauce over fish.

****

Haddock Cakes

1 lb. cooked haddock
1 medium onion, finely chopped
1 1/2 cups mushrooms, chopped
2 cups bread crumbs
1 tsp. seasoned salt
1/4 cup parsley, chopped
2 eggs, beaten
3 Tbsp. butter
2 Tbsp. oil
Lemon wedges (optional)

1. Remove bones from fish.

2. Flake completely by hand.

3. Place in a mixing bowl.

4. Add chopped onion and mushrooms.

5. Stir in 1 cup bread crumbs, salt, parsley, and eggs.

6. Form into patties and add more bread crumbs if needed to bind.

7. Coat patties with remaining bread crumbs.

8. Heat butter and oil in skillet, then fry patties on each side. Serve with tartar sauce.

Spicy Haddock Snacks

1 1/2 lbs. haddock fillets,
1/4 cup celery, chopped
1 cup onion, chopped
1/4 cup green pepper, chopped
1/4 stick butter
1 egg
2 Tbsp. seafood seasoning
1 Tbsp. oregano
1 1/2 tsp. garlic powder
1 1/2 tsp. Tabasco sauce
1 Tbsp. Worcestershire sauce
2 Tbsp. mayonnaise
2 cups cracker crumbs

1. Sauté celery, onion and pepper in butter until tender.

2. Put in bowl and add fish, egg, seafood seasoning, oregano, garlic powder, Tabasco sauce and Worcestershire sauce. Mix well.

3. Add mayonnaise and cracker crumbs until mixture is just firm enough to roll into small balls that hold together.

4. Deep fry at 375° F. until light brown.

Baked Haddock

1 lb. haddock fillets
1 small onion, thinly sliced
Salt and pepper
5 Tbsp. butter, melted
2 Tbsp. lemon juice
3/4 cup white wine
1/2 cup water
Oregano
1 small can sliced mushrooms
2 green onions, chopped

1. Arrange onion slices in bottom of buttered shallow pan.

2. Rub fillets with salt and pepper, and arrange over onions; brush fish with melted butter.

3. Combine wine, lemon juice and water, and pour around fillets.

4. Sprinkle with oregano then cover with sliced mushrooms and chopped green onions.

5. Bake in a 400° F. oven for about 20 minutes, basting with liquid in pan.

****

160

Broiled Haddock

1 lb. haddock fillets
2 Tbsp. butter, melted
1/2 tsp. salt
1/4 tsp. pepper

1. Brush fillets with melted butter and season with the salt and pepper.

2. Place on a well-buttered broiler, and broil until it flakes with a fork.

3. Turn and broil other side briefly.

4. Serve with garnish.

Fried Halibut

2 lbs. halibut fillets
1 tsp. salt
Dash of pepper
1 egg
1 Tbsp. milk
1 cup fine cracker crumbs

1. Cut fillets into serving pieces.

2. Sprinkle both sides with salt and pepper.

3. Beat egg slightly and blend with milk.

4. Dip fish in egg and roll in crumbs.

5. Fry fish in a basket at about 375° F. for 3 to 5 minutes.

Easy Poached Halibut

3 lbs. halibut fillets
3 cups milk
1 medium onion, sliced
Salt and pepper to taste

1. Soak halibut in the milk for 4 hours before cooking.

2. Place the onion rings on top of the fish and milk and bake at 350° F. for 15 to 20 minutes or until fish flakes with a fork.

Canadian Halibut Chowder

1 lb. halibut
Onions
1/2 cup long grain rice
1 Tbsp. flour
Potatoes
Celery
Cabbage
Garlic
Curry
Carrots

1.   Cook vegetables and rice.

2.   Cut halibut into small pieces.

3.   When vegetables are nearly done, add halibut.

4.   Add curry and garlic.

5.   Add enough water to cover halibut and vegetables.

6.   Add 2 Tbsp. flour to thicken. Do not boil.

****

Fishing stories haven't changed in 2500 years. The Greeks, too, used to listen to lyres.

Baked Stuffed Halibut

4 5-oz. halibut fillets
3-oz. crab meat
3-oz. shrimp
3-oz. Brie cheese, cut into small cubes
1 Tbsp. fresh dill, chopped
1/8 tsp. salt
1/8 tsp. pepper
3 Tbsp. mayonnaise

1. Pre-heat oven to 400° F.

2. Slit the halibut fillets lengthwise to form a pocket for stuffing. Set aside.

3. In a mixing bowl, combine crab, shimp, cheese, dill, salt and pepper.

4. Fold in mayonnaise to bind mixture.

5. Divide stuffing among the four pocketed fillets, covering the stuffing with flaps.

6. Bake in a lightly buttered baking dish about 12 minutes.

Courtesy Georgeann Lang, Indianapolis, Indiana.

Lobster Au Gratin

2 Lobster tails
3 Tbsp. butter
6 Tbsp. flour
1/2 Tbsp. salt
1/8 tsp. pepper
2 cups milk
1 cup cheese, grated

1. In saucepan bring 4 cups water to boil.

2. Add two whole lobster tails and boil for 5 minutes. Remove and drain water immediately. Cut into 1-inch pieces.

3. Melt butter in skillet.

4. Add flour, salt and pepper, stirring until smooth.

5. Add milk gradually and cook until thick, stirring constantly.

6. Arrange lobster pieces in a medium casserole. Cover with sauce and top with cheese.

7. Bake at 350° F. for 30 - 35 minutes.

****

Lobster Bisque

1 8-oz. can lobster or fresh lobster
Sherry wine
3 to 4 green onions, chopped
2 Tbsp. butter
1 10 1/2-oz. can tomato soup
1 can milk
1 10 1/2-oz. can cream of mushroom soup
1 can half & half cream
Pinch of thyme
Chopped parsley

1. Finely mince lobster; marinate in wine.

2. Sauté onions in butter.

3. Add lobster meat and cook for a few minutes.

4. Combine soups, milk, thyme and parsley.

5. Add lobster and simmer for a few minutes.

****

Lobster Thermidor

2 cups cubed cooked lobster meat
1/4 cup butter
2 Tbsp. cognac
3 Tbsp. dry sherry
1 cup heavy cream, scalded
3 egg yolks, beaten
Salt and freshly ground black pepper to taste
1/8 tsp. cayenne pepper.

1. Melt the butter, add the lobster meat and cook three minutes. Shake the pan or stir while cooking.

2. Add the cognac and sherry.

3. Pour the cream over the egg yolks and add to lobster mixture.

4. Reheat, stirring, until mixture thickens, but do not allow to boil.

5. Season with salt, pepper and cayenne.

****

Lobster Newburg

2 lbs. lobster meat
1/4 cup butter
Salt and pepper
1/4 tsp. nutmeg, grated
1 Tbsp. sherry wine
1 Tbsp. brandy
1/3 cup cream
2 egg yolks

1.   Cut lobster in slices.

2.   Melt butter, add lobster and cook 3 minutes.

3.   Add all seasonings and cook 1 minute.

4.   Add cream and egg yolks slightly beaten.

5.   Stir until thickened. Do not boil.

****

Barney Mildew and his wife were out in a boat at dawn. The air was raw. Bugs were everywhere. His wife said, "Tell me again what a good time I'm having. I keep forgetting!"

Snapper Snacks

4 6-oz. red snapper fillets
Flour, to dredge
2 Tbsp. oil
4 Tbsp. butter
1/2 cup parsley, minced
1/4 cup fresh lemon juice
1 clove garlic, peeled, finely minced
Salt and pepper to taste
Lemon wedges, for garnish

1. Cut each fillet into 1 1/2-inch pieces.

2. Dredge each in flour, pressing flour evenly into fish, then shaking off excess.

3. Heat wok. Add oil and butter. When butter melts and begins to sizzle add a few fish pieces at a time.

4. Cook quickly over medium heat, turning until pieces are lightly browned on both sides.

5. Remove and set aside.

6. Add garlic to oil and butter. Stir-fry about 15 seconds. Remove wok from heat.

7. Add fish, salt, pepper, parsley and lemon juice. Toss fish briefly in mixture.

Alaska Salmon Melts

1 can (14 1/2-oz.) salmon
1/3 cup mayonnaise
2 Tbsp. parsley, minced
2 Tbsp. onion, minced
2 Tbsp. pimento, drained and chopped
2 tsp. lemon juice
3/4 cup cheddar cheese, shredded and divided
8 slices French bread
Dash pepper

1. Drain salmon; break into large chunks.

2. Add mayonnaise, parsley, onion, pimento, lemon juice and pepper toss gently to mix.

3. Fold in 1/2 cup cheese.

4. Spread about 1/4 cup mixture on each slice of bread.

5. Sprinkle remaining cheese over salmon mixture.

6. Broil about 6-inches from heat 3 to 4 minutes or until cheese melts and tops are golden.

****

Angler: A delusion entirely surrounded by liars in old clothes.

Salmon Soup

1 can (14 1/2-oz) salmon
1 pint milk
1/2 tsp. salt
2 Tbsp. butter
Dash of pepper

1. Melt butter in a pan.

2. Add milk, salt, pepper.

3. Add salmon and simmer for 5 to 10 minutes.

Courtesy Gloria Bradway, Warsaw, Indiana

Hearty Salmon Loaf

1 can (14 1/2-oz) pink salmon
4 Tbsp. mayonnaise
2 tsp. lemon juice
4 Tbsp. celery, finely chopped
2 Tbsp. onion, finely chopped
1/2 tsp. salt
Dash pepper
1 cup bread crumbs
2 large eggs, slightly beaten
1 1/2 cup peas in white sauce

1.   In small bowl, combine first 3 ingredients.

2.   Add next 4 ingredients, stir in bread crumbs and
     eggs.

3.   Mix well; shape into loaf, place on greased 1 qt.
     baking dish.

4.   Bake 25 minutes in preheated 350° F. oven.

5.   Spoon warm peas over loaf.

****

Give a man a fish, and he'll eat for a day.
Teach a man to fish, and the old buzzard won't be
hanging around underfoot all the time.

Wife of retired executive

Salmon Croquettes

1 4-oz. can salmon
1 slice bread, crumbled in blender
3-oz. skim milk
Dash parsley flakes
1 Tbsp. dehydrated onion flakes
Salt and pepper (to taste)

1. Combine all ingredients; mix well and shape into cone-shaped croquettes.

2. Bake at 350° F. for 20 minutes on a non-stick cookie sheet. Serves 2 for lunch.

****

A man stopped his car on a bridge and called down to the fisherman below. "Any luck?"

"No," the man said as he reeled in his lure. "But you should have been here yesterday. I caught 40 bass."

"You don't say," said the spectator. "Did you happen to know that I'm the game warden in this county?"

"Sure enough," replied the fisherman, "and I'm the biggest liar in this county!"

Grilled Steamed Salmon

3 to 5 lbs. salmon fillets
1/4 cup water
Sliced onion
3 Tbsp. butter
Salt
Pepper
Paprika

1. Place salmon in heavy duty aluminum foil tent.

2. Add water, sliced onions, butter.

3. Sprinkle with salt, pepper and paprika to taste.

4. Seal the foil tent and place on the grill.

5. Grill for about 20 to 30 minutes. Steam should be able to escape a little from the top.

6. Serve with lemon, salt and pepper.

Courtesy Wayne Kubek, Lansing, Illinois.

****

There is no use in driving 100 miles to fish when you can be just as unsuccessful near home.

Salmon Steak in Foil

6 1-inch salmon steaks
1 cup olive oil
2 Tbsp. onion, chopped
2 Tbsp. parsley
2 Tbsp. lemon juice
Salt and pepper to taste
6 thin slices of bacon

1. Mix marinade of oil, lemon juice, onion and parsley.

2. Pour over salmon and soak overnight.

3. Pre-heat oven to 425° F.

4. Grease foil and add the salmon, bacon slices and a tablespoon of marinade.

5   Close foil. Bake about 20 minutes.

****

"Oh dear, " the vacationing wife said to her husband. "Do you have another cork in your tackle box? This one keep sinking."

Salmon Pancakes

1 can (7 3/4-oz.) salmon, drained and flaked
1 cup pancake mix
1 egg
1 cup milk
1 Tbsp. salad oil
White sauce, prepared in advance*

* See pages 50 - 51.

1. Combine all ingredients except the salmon and the sauce.

2. Stir the batter until smooth, add half of salmon.

3. Heat pancake griddle or frying pan, oil it lightly and fry each pan cake until golden brown on both sides.

4. Add remaining salmon to the prepared white sauce and serve over hot pancakes.

****

Why do fish have scales? So they can weigh themselves.

Pacific Salmon Loaf

1 16-ounce can salmon, drained and flaked
1/4 cup celery, chopped
1/4 cup green pepper, chopped
1/2 cup onion, chopped
1/2 cup dry bread crumbs
1/2 cup Kraft Real Mayonnaise
1 egg, beaten
1 tsp. salt
Cucumber sauce*

* See page 49, cucumber sauce A.

1. Combine ingredients except cucumber sauce;
    mix lightly.

2. Shape into loaf in shallow baking dish.

3. Bake at 350° F. for 40 minutes.

****

Good fishing is just a matter of timing. You have to
get there by yesterday.

Salmonburgers

1 can (15 1/2-oz.) Alaska salmon
1 Tbsp. lemon juice
1 egg, slightly beaten
1/2 cup onion, chopped
1/2 cup green pepper, finely chopped
1/2 cup fresh whole wheat crumbs
1 tsp. lemon peel, grated
1/2 tsp. rosemary, crushed
1/8 tsp. pepper

1.   Drain salmon and flake.

2.   Combine ingredients. Mix well.

3.   Form into 4 or 5 patties.

4.   Pan-fry in small amount of vegetable oil until
      lightly browned on both sides.

5.   Serve on toasted hamburger buns.

****

There are sport fishermen, and then there are those
who catch fish!

Salmon Casserole

1 can (15 1/2-oz.) salmon
1/2 cup onion, chopped
2 Tbsp. butter
1 can cream of celery soup
2/3 cup milk
1/2 cup sharp cheddar cheese, grated
2 Tbsp. parmesan cheese, grated
1 tsp. salt
4 tsp. pepper
1 tsp. dry mustard
1 pkg. frozen peas

1.   Sauté onion in butter.

2.   Add soup, milk, cheeses and seasonings.

3.   Stir until cheeses melt.

4.   Separate salmon, leaving in chunks and
     removing bones.

5.   Thaw peas slightly to separate.

6.   Combine all ingredients and pour into greased
     2 1/2 quart casserole.

7.   Bake at 350° F. for 30 to 40 minutes.

Salmon-stuffed Tomatoes

1 can (15 1/2-oz.) salmon
1 cup cucumber, pared and diced
1 Tbsp. onion, chopped
1 Tbsp. pimento, chopped
1 cup mayonnaise
6 medium tomatoes, chilled
1 tsp. salt
Dash pepper

1. Break salmon in small chunks, removing bones and skin.

2. Combine salmon with cucumber, onion, seasonings, pimento, and mayonnaise. Chill.

3. Scoop out centers of tomatoes to make cups.

4. Fill with salmon mixture. Serve on lettuce.

****

There's nothing a fisherman can do if his worm ain't trying!

180

Salmon Nuggets

1 can (15 1/2-oz.) salmon
2 cups potatoes, mashed
1 Tbsp. celery, finely minced
1 Tbsp. butter, melted
1 Tbsp. onion, grated
1 cup dry bread crumbs
1 1/2 tsp. Worcestershire sauce
1 egg, beaten
1/4 tsp. salt
Dash of pepper
1/4 lb. sharp cheese

1.   Drain and flake salmon.

2.   Combine all ingredients except cheese and mix
     thoroughly.

3.   Shape into balls the size of walnuts.

4.   Cut cheese into 3/8-in. cubes and insert a cube
     into the center of each fish ball.

5.   Reshape balls and roll in bread crumbs.

6.   Fry in deep fat at 375° F. 3 - 4 minutes or until
     golden brown. Garnish and serve hot, plain or
     with a mustard sauce.

Courtesy Charles Badai, Anchorage, Alaska.

Smoked Salmon Spread

1 lb. smoked salmon (or regular salmon plus 1 tsp.
   liquid smoke)
1 lb. cream cheese
1/4 cup fresh parsley, chopped
2 Tbsp. onion, minced
1/8 tsp. hot pepper sauce
1 clove garlic, minced
2 tsp. capers, chopped

1. Combine all ingredients and mix well.

2. Chill 4 hours.

Courtesy Charles Badai, Anchorage, Alaska.

Orange Roughy in Sauce

2 orange roughy fillets (about 6-oz. each)
2 Tbsp. butter
1/4 cup fresh orange juice
1 Tbsp. fresh lime juice
Salt

1.   In large skillet, melt butter over medium heat.

2. Add fillets. Cook until fish flakes easily when tested with a fork, turning once.

3. Remove fillets to serving platter.

4. Add orange juice and lime juice to liquid in skillet. Boil rapidly, stirring constantly, to reduce juices to about 1/4 cup.

5. Add salt and pepper to taste.

6. Pour pan juices over fillets.

Oyster Soup

20 small oysters
2 cups skim milk
1/2 lb. cream cheese
2 cups chicken stock
1/2 onion, finely chopped
1/2 green pepper, finely chopped
1 1/2 tsp. salt
1/4 tsp. pepper
Celery leaves, chopped

1. Blend together the skim milk and cream cheese in a saucepan.

2. Add the remaining ingredients and heat thoroughly. Do not boil.

3. Serve garnished with chopped celery leaves.

Maryland Scalloped Oysters

1 pint oysters, drain, save liquor
2 cups cracker crumbs
1/2 tsp. butter, melted
1/2 tsp. salt
3/4 cup cream
1/4 cup oyster liquor
1/2 tsp. Worcestershire sauce
Dash of pepper

1. Combine crumbs, butter, salt and pepper.

2. Pour melted butter over crumbs; stir.

3. Spread 1/3 in greased 8" by 1 1/2" round pan.

4. Cover with 1/2 of oysters; use another 1/3 of crumbs and remaining oysters.

5. Combine cream, oyster liquor and Worchestershire sauce.

6. Pour over oysters just before putting them in the oven.

7. Add remaining bread crumbs.

8. Bake at 350° F. for 40 - 45 minutes. Serve at once.

Maine Curried Oysters

1 qt. oysters
2 tsp. curry powder
2 Tbsp. butter
1/4 pint oyster liquor
1/4 pint milk
1/2 tsp. onion juice
1 Tbsp. flour
1 tsp. salt

1. Heat onion juice in pan, add flour and curry powder and when mixture bubbles, stir in oyster liquor, milk and salt.

2. When sauce is smooth and boils, put in oysters and cook about 4 minutes or until they are plump and edges crimp.

****

I fished in a Texas lake that was so crowded with fish they had to swim standing up!

Fried Oysters

1 qt. oysters
1 cup bread crumbs
2 eggs, beaten
1 cup cracker crumbs or corn meal
2 Tbsp. milk
Salt and pepper

1.   Drain oysters.

2.   Mix eggs, milk, seasonings.

3.   Dip oysters in egg mixture and roll in crumbs.

4.   Fry in oil at 375° F. about 2 minutes or
     until brown.

****

A fisherman returned to shore with a giant marlin
that was bigger and heavier than he. On the way to
the cleaning shed, he ran into a second fisherman
who had a string of a dozen baby minnows. The
second fisherman looked at the marlin, turned to the
first fisherman, and asked, "Only caught the one,
eh?"

Toasted Sardine Sandwiches

2 cans sardines
12 slices white bread
6 slices cheese (1-oz. each)
1/3 cup soft butter or margarine

1. Drain the liquid off the sardines.

2. Cut the sardines in half the long way.

3. Put the sardines on 6 slices of bread.

4. Put a slice of cheese on top of the sardines.

5. Cover with a slice of bread.

6. Spread butter on the outside of the sandwiches.

7. Fry the sandwiches for 4 to 5 minutes or until brown.

8. Turn the sandwiches carefully. Fry 4 to 5 minutes more or until brown.

****

"Are the fish biting today?"
"If they are---only one another!"

Deviled Scallops

2 lb. scallops, halved
1/4 cup boiling water
1/2 cup butter
1/2 cup milk
1 Tbsp. flour
1 1/2 tsp. prepared mustard
3/4 tsp. salt
Dash cayenne pepper
2 cups fresh bread crumbs
2 Tbsp. butter, melted

1. Heat oven to 350° F.

2. Boil scallops in water 3 minutes; drain.

3. In saucepan, combine butter, flour, mustard, salt, and pepper; slowly stir in milk; cook over low heat just till thickened.

4. Add scallops then place into 10" by 6" by 2" baking dish.

5. Top with combined crumbs and butter.

6. Bake 20 to 25 minutes.

****

Zesty Fried Scallops

1 lb. scallops
2 eggs
1 Tbsp. lemon juice
1 cup fine dry bread crumbs
1/2 tsp. thyme
1/2 tsp. tarragon
1/2 tsp. dill
1/2 tsp. parsley
Vegetable oil
Tartar sauce

1.   Clean and rinse scallops. Dry completely on
     paper towels.

2.   Beat eggs well.

3.   Add lemon juice.

4.   Select herbs (thyme, tarragon or dill) you wish
     to use and mix with bread crumbs.

5.   Dip scallops in crumbs, in egg mixture, then in
     crumbs again.

6.   Heat 1/4-inch of oil in frying pan.

7.   Fry scallops about 3 minutes on each side until
     golden. Drain on paper towels.

Scallops with Bacon

4 cups scallops
Water
1/2 pound thinly sliced bacon

1. Preheat oven to 350° F.

2. Place scallops and water to cover in saucepan;
   bring to a boil. Boll just until scallops begin to
   shrink then drain.

3. Cover bottom of baking pan with layer of bacon.
   Add all the scallops; cover with remaining
   bacon. Bake until bacon is crisp.

4. Remove from oven, and serve at once.

Garlic Buttered Scallops

1 lb. scallops
1/3 cup butter
1 clove garlic, split
2 Tbsp. green onions
1 Tbsp. parsley, chopped
1 tsp. oregano
3 Tbsp. lemon juice
Salt and pepper

3 Tbsp. lemon juice
Salt and pepper

1.   Wash and pat scallops dry with absorbent
     paper.

2.   Brown the garlic in butter.

3.   Remove garlic, mix butter with seasonings.

4.   Place scallops in baking dish.

5.   Pour butter mixture over them.

6.   Broil about 5 minutes, until scallops are done.

7.   Add lemon juice.

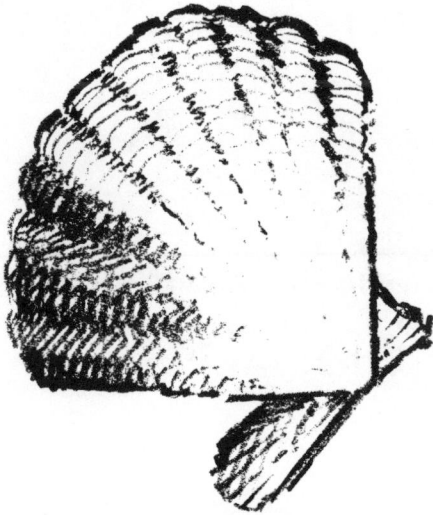

Seaburgers

1 7-oz. can each lobster, crab, salmon, and tuna
1/2 lb. processed sharp cheese
1/4 cup onion
1/2 cup sweet pickle, chopped
1/2 cup catsup
1/4 cup mayonnaise
1 cup celery, minced
2 tsp. salt
1/2 tsp. pepper
2 Tbsp. pimento, minced
12 buns

1.   Preheat oven to 350° F.

2.   Mix all ingredients.

3.   Bake for 20 minutes and serve on buns.

****

"So God created the great creatures of the sea and every living and moving thing with which the water teems, according to their kinds...And God saw that it was good." Genesis 1:21 (NIV)

Seafood Soup

1/2 lb. shrimp, shelled, deveined and cut in half cross-
    wise
1/2 lb. sea scallops, coarsely chopped
1 16-oz. can whole new potatoes, drained and
    diced
1 clove garlic, crushed
1/4 cup butter or margarine
2/3 cup all-purpose flour
2 13 3/4 fluid oz. cans chicken broth
1/2 tsp. ground white pepper
1 cup light cream or half-and-half

1. In large saucepan, over medium heat, cook
    shrimp, scallops, potatoes and garlic in
    margarine until seafood is done.

2. Stir in flour until blended. Gradually add
    chicken broth and pepper. Heat to a boil,
    stirring constantly. Boil 1 minute.

3. Stir in light cream; heat through. Do not boil.

            ****

It shakes you up a little bit when you open a can of
sardines and fifty eyes look up at you!

Zesty Fried Prawns

2 lbs. raw prawns
2 eggs, beaten
3 cups peanut oil
1 cup cracker crumbs
1/2 cup flour
1/2 tsp. curry powder
1/8 tsp. salt
Chili sauce

1. Peel prawns and de-vein; wipe with a damp cloth; split open lengthwise; spread apart lengthwise.

2. Sift flour, curry powder, and salt into mixing bowl; add cracker crumbs.

3. Dip prawns into eggs beaten until foamy, then roll in seasoned flour mixture.

4. Pour peanut oil into large skillet; heat but do not allow to smoke (about 350° F.).

5   Fry prawns 3 minutes, or until golden brown.

6. Drain on absorbent paper. Serve on preheated plates with chili sauce.

Maine Shrimp Bisque

1 lb. fresh shrimp
4 cups milk
1 bay leaf
2 slices onion
1 cup celery, diced
3 Tbsp. parsley, chopped
1/3 cup butter
1/3 cup flour
3/4 tsp. salt
1/8 tsp. pepper

1. Wash shrimp thoroughly in cold running water; put into rapidly boiling salted water; cover; boil 15 minutes; drain.

2. Remove from shells and take out black vein. Chop into tiny pieces.

3. Pour milk into saucepan; add bay leaf, onion slices, celery, and parsley.

4. Scald milk about 2 minutes; do not boil.

5. Melt butter in deep saucepan over low flame; stir in flour, salt, and pepper.

6.   When very smooth, gradually add scalded milk, add shrimp stirring constantly until mixture boils. Cook 5 minutes, stirring constantly.

Bacon Wrapped Shrimp Snacks

1 lb. shrimp
1/4 cup soy sauce
1 Tbsp. sugar
1 small clove garlic, minced
1 tsp. ginger root, grated
7 - 8 slices bacon

1.   Combine soy sauce, sugar, garlic, ginger root, and dash pepper; let stand 1 hour at room temperature.

2.   Cut bacon slices in thirds. Wrap piece of bacon around each shrimp; skewer to secure.

3.   Grill bacon-wrapped shrimp over hot coals about 15 minutes or till done, turning and brushing with soy mixture frequently.

****

Curried Shrimp

2 lb. cleaned cooked fresh shrimp
1/2 cup green pepper, chopped
1/3 cup butter
1/2 cup onion, chopped
2 cloves garlic, minced
2 cups sour cream
2 tsp. curry powder
3/4 tsp. salt
Dash of chill powder
2 tsp. lemon juice

1.   Sauté shrimp, pepper, butter, onion, and garlic together.

2.   Stir in sour cream, lemon juice, curry powder, salt, and chili powder.

3.   Serve with rice.

****

One of my goldfish wasn't moving too well, so I called up the local university and asked one of the ichthyologists what the problem was. He said, "It sounds like rheumatism. Keep that fish out of damp places!"

Summer Shrimp Snack

2 small cans shrimp, drained
1/2 cup celery, chopped fine
1/4 lb. butter
8-oz. cream cheese
2 tsp. lemon juice
1 small onion, chopped
2 tsp. mayonnaise
Dash of garlic salt
Dash of Worcestershire sauce
Salt and pepper or Lowry's seasoned salt.

1.   Mix all ingredients until smooth.

2.   Serve with crackers, potato chips or party rye.

Shrimp-Curry Salad

3 cups cooked, cleaned shrimp or lobster meat
3 cups cooked rice
2 cups cooked or canned peas
2 cups celery, slivered
1/2 cup chutney
1 1/2 tsp. salt
3/4 cup French dressing
1/2 to 1 tsp. curry powder
Salad greens

1. Combine all ingredients except greens.

2. Toss; refrigerate. Serve on greens.

Spicy Hot Shrimp

4 Tbsp. butter, room temperature
36 large shrimp, cleaned, deveined
1 8-oz. can tomato sauce
4 or 5 drops red-hot pepper sauce
1/4 cup lemon juice
1 tsp. Worcestershire sauce
1 Tbsp. bottled horseradish
2 to 3 cups hot cooked rice or 4 to 6 pieces of toast
Salt to taste

1. Heat wok. Add butter and melt over medium high heat.

2. When butter begins to sizzle, add shrimp. Stir-fry about 5 minutes until shrimp are firm and pink.

3. Add remaining ingredients and stir until bubbly hot.

4. Serve over rice or with toast.

Fiery Cajun Shrimp

5 - 6 lbs raw shrimp in shells
1 sticks melted butter
1 sticks melted margarine
1/2 cup Worcestershire sauce
4 Tbsp. black pepper
2 tsp. Tabasco sauce
4 cloves garlic, minced
Juice of 2 lemons
2 lemons, sliced

1. Heat oven to 400° F.

2. Mix all ingredients except shrimp and lemon slices.

3. Pour 1/2 of sauce in bottom of baking pan.

4. Arrange shrimp and lemon slices in layers.

5. Pour remaining sauce on top.

6. Bake uncovered for 15 to 20 minutes stirring once or twice.

7. Serve with hard crust bread to dip in sauce.

Courtesy Dolly Chapel, Warsaw, Indiana.

Barbecued Shrimp

1 1/2 lbs. shrimp, washed and shelled
2 onions, chopped
2 sprigs celery, chopped fine
1 tsp. salt
Dash of pepper
1 clove garlic, minced
1/2 cup parsley, chopped
1/3 cup olive or vegetable oil
1 Tbsp. wine vinegar
1 cup tomato sauce
1/2 cup water

1.   Sauté onion, celery and seasonings in olive oil,
      stirring constantly until soft and golden.

2.   Add shrimp, and stir over moderate heat until
      moisture is absorbed.

3.   Add wine vinegar, or 4 Tbsp. white wine,
      then tomato sauce and water.

4.   Cook about 15 minutes. (A bay leaf may be
      added for extra flavor).

****

Cream Puffs and Shrimp

1 lb. fresh, shelled shrimp
1/2 cup celery, chopped
1/3 cup mayonnaise
1 1/2 tsp. lemon juice
Salt and pepper

1.   Bake 4-inch oblong puffs.

2.   Boil shrimp 3 - 5 minutes or until done.

3.   Chill shrimp.

4.   Mix shrimp with all ingredients.

5.   Line cream puffs with lettuce then add shrimp
     mixture.

Courtesy Dolly Chapel, Warsaw, Indiana.

****

The waiter served the fish entree. The diner took
one bite and asked, "What is this?"
   The waiter said, "Filet of sole, sir."
   "Well," the diner replied, "take it back and see if
you can get me a softer part of the shoe!"

Seaman's Stew

2 lbs. firm-fleshed white fish (cod, haddock or halibut), cut in large chunks
2 onions, sliced
2 Tbsp. vegetable oil
3 6-oz. cans Hunt's Tomato Paste
3 cups water
1/2 tsp. each: red pepper and black pepper
1 cup parsley, finely chopped
1/3 cup dry white wine
6 slices of Italian bread (toasted, if desired)
1/2 tsp. salt

1. Sprinkle fish with 1/2 tsp. salt; let stand 1 hour.

2. Meanwhile, lightly brown onion in hot oil;
   drain.

3. Stir in water, Hunt's Tomato Paste, red pepper,
   black pepper, 1 1/2 tsp. salt, parsley and wine.

4. Simmer 20 minutes.

5. Add fish, simmer about 10 minutes longer or
   just until fish flakes easily with a fork.

6. To serve, place a slice of bread in each soup
   bowl; ladle soup over.

Tuna Patties

1 medium zucchini, finely chopped
1 can tuna, drained
1 1/2 cup bread crumbs
2 eggs
1/4 cup onion, chopped
1 tsp. lemon juice
Salt and pepper to taste

1.   Mix all ingredients well.

2.   Shape into 15 patties.

3.   Fry in hot oil until brown on both sides.

Tuna-Cashew Casserole

1 can cream of mushroom soup, undiluted
1/4 cup water
1 can chunk-style tuna
1/4 lb. cashew nuts
1 cup celery, finely diced
1/4 cup onion, minced
Salt and pepper to taste
1 3-oz. jar chow mein noodles

1. Combine all ingredients, reserving some nood-
    les.

2. Place in casserole.

3. Sprinkle remaining noodles on top.

4. Bake at 325° F. for 40 minutes.

****

When I was first married, my wife made salmon
dishes three times a week----salmon salad, salmon
croquettes, salmon steak, poached salmon. When
spring came, I had to resist an urge to go north and
spawn!

Tuna Casserole

2 cans tuna
1 pkg. macaroni
3 Tbsp. butter
2 Tbsp. flour
1 1/4 cup milk
1 can cream of chicken soup
1 small onion, chopped
1 small green pepper, chopped
1 pimento, cut up
Buttered bread crumbs

1.   Cook macaroni according to package directions; drain.

2.   Combine butter, flour and milk to make sauce.

3.   Add remaining ingredients except crumbs.

4.   Place in casserole; cover with crumbs.

5.   Bake about 45 minutes at 350° F.

****

Fish must be brain food, because they travel in schools!

Tuna Burgers

1 7-oz. can tuna
3/4 cup celery, finely chopped
1/2 cup yellow cheese, diced
1 small onion, chopped
1/3 cup mayonnaise
Salt and pepper to taste

1.   Mix all ingredients.

2.   Fill buttered buns with tuna.

3.   Wrap in foil and place in oven for 15 minutes at
     350° F.

Tuna Cheese Spread

2 3-oz pkgs. cream cheese.
2 Tbsp. lemon juice
1 16-oz. can chunk tuna, drained and mashed
1/4 cup pimento-stuffed green olives, sliced
1/4 cup almonds, chopped
1/4 cup sweet pickles, finely chopped
1/3 cup celery, finely chopped
1/4 cup green onions, thinly sliced
3 English muffins

1. *Beat the cream cheese and lemon until fluffy.*

2. *Stir in the rest of the ingredients.*

3. *Toast and butter the English muffins.*

4. *Place a small piece of lettuce on each muffin half and spread with tuna mixture.*

Other Menu Items

The following coleslaw recipe is one of the best. It was served at the old Trolly Bar in Fort Wayne, Indiana, and always brought praise from its customers.

Cartwight's Coleslaw

1 medium head cabbage (about 2 lbs.)
1 medium carrot
1 small onion
3/4 cup Kraft Mayonnaise
3/4 cup sugar
1/4 tsp. salt
3/4 tsp. pimentos, chopped

1. Shred fine cabbage, carrot and onion.

2. Combine with Kraft Mayonnaise (salad dressing won't work, the chef insisted), sugar, salt and chopped pimentos.

3. Mix well. Store in refrigerator at least 2 hours.

****

Fat Fish and Lean Fish

The lists below evaluate only those fish utilized in this book. They are all categorized as either: high in fat, moderately fatty, or lean.

Freshwater Fish

High in Fat

Lake trout
Rainbow trout
Salmon
Brook trout
Smelt
Shad

Moderately Fatty

Whitefish
White perch
Yellow bass

Lean Fish

Carp
Yellow Perch
Catfish
Sauger

Lean Fish (Con't)

Walleye
Saugeye
Muskie
Pickerel
Northern pike
Bluegills
Crappies

Rock bass
Pumpkinseed
Largemouth bass
Smallmouth bass
Longear sunfish
Warmouth

Redear sunfish
Green sunfish
White bass
Suckers

Saltwater Fish

High in Fat

Anchovies
Bluefish
Kingfish
Herring
Sardines
Mackerel
Albacore
Yellowfin tuna
Spotted sea trout
Shad
Smelt
Salmon

Moderately Fatty

Weakfish
Mullet
Sheepshead
Striped bass

Lean Fish

Cod
Haddock
Pollock

Lean Fish (Con't)

Flounder
Halibut
Sole
Black sea bass
Grouper
Red snapper

Equivalent Measurements

A pinch......................1/8 teaspoon or less
3 teaspoons............................ 1 tablespoon
4 tablespoons.................................. 1/4 cup
8 tablespoons.................................. 1/2 cup
12 tablespoons................................ 3/4 cup
16 tablespoons................................... 1 cup
2 cups.. 1 pint
4 cups.. 1 quart
4 quarts....................................... 1 gallon
8 quarts... 1 peck
4 pecks... 1 bushel
16 ounces..................................... 1 pound
32 ounces...................................... 1 quart
8 ounces liquid.................................. 1 cup
1 ounce liquid......................... 2 tablespoons

(For liquid and dry measurements use
standard measuring spoons and cups.
All measurements are level.)

Index

Sauces

Flavored Butters

Batters

Freshwater Fish

Other Menu Items

Fat Fish and Lean Fish 210

Equivalent Measurements 212

Order Form

The "Real Fishermen" series by John Davis is a popular collection of humorous stories involving such wacky characters as Sam Splitshot, Willie Woodslab, Waldo Hornripple and many more. Every topic from Asparagus to Santa Claus is treated in such a way that even a grouch will laugh.

Number	Title	Price	Total
_____	Real Fishermen Are Never Thin	$7.95	_____
_____	Real Fishermen Never Lie	$7.95	_____
_____	Real Fishermen Never Wear Suits	$7.95	_____

(All 3 books only $25 P & H included!)   TOTAL   _____

20% P & H   _____

☐ I would like my books
autographed by the author.   TOTAL   _____

Order From:

Pinegrove Publishing
P.O. Box 557
Winona Lake, IN 46590

Ship to:

Name:_____

Address:_____

_____

_____Zip_____

Order Form

Please send me _____ copies of John Davis' <u>Fish and Seafood Recipe Book</u> at $17.95 per copy plus $2.50 for shipping and handling. Enclosed is my check or money order for $_____

□ I would like my book(s) autographed by the author.

<u>Order from:</u>

     Pinegrove Publishing
     P.O. Box 557
     Winona Lake, IN 46590

<u>Ship to:</u>

Name:_____

Address:_____

_____

_____ Zip_____